The Economics of Preferential Trade Agreements

Edited by Jagdish Bhagwati and Arvind Panagariya

The AEI Press
Publisher for the American Enterprise Institute
Washington, D.C.

Center for International Economics
University of Maryland
College Park

1996

Library of Congress Cataloging-in-Publication Data

The economics of preferential trade agreements / edited by Jagdish
   Bhagwati and Arvind Panagariya.
     p. cm.
   Includes bibliographical references and index.
   ISBN 0-8447-3968-5 (cloth).—ISBN 978-0-8447-3969-4 (pbk)
    1. Tariff preferences—United States.   2. Trade blocks—United
States.   3. United States—Commercial policy.   I. Bhagwati, Jagdish
N., 1934- .   II. Panagariya, Arvind.
HF1731.E25   1996
382'.973—dc20   96-41434
                                                        CIP

THE AEI PRESS
Publisher for the American Enterprise Institute
1150 17th Street, N.W., Washington, D.C. 20036

The Economics
of Preferential
Trade Agreements

To John and Mary Ruggie,
intellectuals and friends
—Jagdish Bhagwati

To my brothers Ravi and Ashok Panagariya
—Arvind Panagariya

Contents

CONTRIBUTORS   xi

PREFACE, *Jagdish Bhagwati and Arvind Panagariya*   xiii
    Exploding Some Popular Claims Favoring PTAs   xiv
    What to Do?   xviii

1 PREFERENTIAL TRADING AREAS AND
    MULTILATERALISM—STRANGERS, FRIENDS, OR FOES?
    Jagdish Bhagwati and Arvind Panagariya   1
    Phrases and Concepts   4
    Rethinking Static Welfare Analysis   5
    Theoretical Analysis of the Dynamic Time-Path
      Question   43
    Implications for Current Policy   52
    Conclusion   55
    Appendix A1: Varieties of PTAs within the World Trade
      Organization   55
    References   74

2 BEYOND NAFTA—THE DESIGN OF A FREE TRADE
    AGREEMENT OF THE AMERICAS, *Paul Wonnacott*   79
    The Historical Background to NAFTA   81
    The Hub-and Spoke Issue   87
    Rules of Origin   90
    Free Trade Agreements Compared with Customs
      Union   92
    Rules of Accession   99
    Where Do We Go from Here?   100
    Conclusions   103
    References   103

3 REGIONALISM AND U.S. TRADE POLICY IN ASIA,
    Gary R. Saxonhouse   108
    Initial U.S. Interest in Preferential Trading
      Arrangements   108

Persistent U.S. Regionalism   109
The Hawke Initiative   109
Conclusion of the Uruguay Round   112
A Pacific Preferential Trading Arrangement   112
Westward Expansion of NAFTA without Japan?   115
The Bogor Declaration   116
Europe's New Asian Trade Policy   118
TAFTA and the New Transatlantic Marketplace   119
APEC's East Asian Members and Reciprocity   121
The Economics and Politics of Unilateral
    Liberalization   125
U.S. Views on East Asian Liberalization   129
Osaka and the Future of APEC   130
Finale   132
References   132

4 REGIONALISM AND U.S. TRADE POLICY, *Claude E. Barfield*   136
The United States—World Trader and Investor   136
The Clinton Trade Policy and Its Critics   139
Multiple FTAs and the Practical World of
    Negotiations   143
Regional Trade Initiatives   145
The Move to Hemispheric Free Trade   145
APEC and the Regional U.S. Focus   149
Europe—A North Atlantic Free Trade Area?   151
The U.S. Political Climate against Further
    Liberalization   153
What Is to Be Done?   155
References   157

INDEX   161

LIST OF FIGURES
1–1   Constant Costs, According to Strictly Vinerian
        Analysis   10
1–2   Effect of Union (A + B) with Rising Costs from
        Partner Country   13
1–3   Effect of Union (A + C) with Rising Costs from
        Outside Country   14
1–4   The Consequences of Differing External Tariff Rates
        in Members of a Free Trade Area   21
1–5   Effect of a Small Tariff Preference by Country A to
        Country B   23

1–6   Effect of Preferential Tariff Reduction and
      Welfare   25
1–7   Example of Positive Effects of Union with a More
      Distant Country   37
1–8   Welfare Loss from Endogenous Increase in External
      Tariff after Formation of a Free Trade Area   40
1–9   Alternative Time-Paths under Multilateralism and
      under PTAs   45
3–1   Relative Size of Nominal Gross Domestic Product,
      in Asia and the Western Hemisphere   110
3–2   Relative Size of the Market for Imports, in Asia and
      the Western Hemisphere   111
3–3   Direct Investment Flows from Japan, the United
      States, and the European Union to East Asia,
      1985–1994   116
3–4   Investment in Manufacturing as a Percentage of
      Total Accumulated Direct Investment by Japanese
      Companies, in Selected East Asian Economies,
      1993   117
3–5   Nominal Tariffs in East Asia, 1978, 1986, and 1991   122
3–6   Average Annual Real Growth Rates, in Various East
      Asian Countries, 1970–1980 and 1980–1993   125
3–7   Average Annual Foreign Direct Investment Inflows
      for Various East Asian Economies, 1982–1992   126
3–8   East Asian Exports, Excluding Japan, to the
      European Union and the United States, 1981 and
      1991   127

LIST OF TABLES

1–1   Gains from Trade under Unilateral Liberalization and
      Free Trade Area   15
1–2   Gains from Trade under Free Trade Area   18
1–3   Direction of Exports by Major Regions, 1980, 1985,
      and 1990   32
A1–1 One Hundred Thirty-Four Regional Trading
      Arrangements Notified to the GATT/WTO,
      1949–1995   56
3–1   Real Gross Domestic Product and Population of
      World and of Members of Major Regional Economic
      Arrangements, 1993   113
3–2   Investment in Manufacturing as Percentage of Total
      Accumulated Direct Investment in Selected East

    Asian Economies by Japanese and American
    Companies, 1993   118

3–3 Effective Rates of Protection for Manufacturing in
     East Asia, Selected Years, 1975–1992   123

3–4 Coverage of Quantitative Restraints on Imports and
     Other Nontariff Barriers, in Korea and Indonesia,
     Selected Years, 1961–1990   124

3–5 Effective Rate of Assistance to Manufacturing,
     Including Nontariff Barriers, in Australia and New
     Zealand, Selected Years, 1970–1988   124

3–6 Ratio of Foreign Direct Investment Inflows to Gross
     Domestic Capital Formation and Ratio of Gross
     Domestic Capital Formation to GDP in East Asia,
     1981–1993   127

3–7 Remaining Restrictions on Foreign Investment
     Maintained by East Asian APEC Members,
     1995   128

3–8 East Asian Bilateral Trade Surpluses, 1992   130

4–1 Trade Patterns of the European Union, NAFTA, and
     Asia, 1983–1993   138

4–2 Snapshot of the Big Emerging Markets, 1994   139

Contributors

CLAUDE E. BARFIELD is a resident scholar at the American Enterprise Institute and the coordinator of its trade policy studies program. He is the editor of many books on trade policy, including most recently *International Financial Markets: Harmonization versus Competition* (AEI Press, 1996), and *Expanding U.S. Asian Trade: New Challenges and Policy Options* (AEI Press, 1996).

JAGDISH BHAGWATI is Arthur Lehman Professor of Economics and professor of political science at Columbia University. He is the author of *Protectionism* (1988) and many other books on trade issues. He recently served as economic policy adviser to the director general of the General Agreement on Tariffs and Trade.

ARVIND PANAGARIYA is professor of economics and codirector of the Center for International Economics at the University of Maryland. He is an editor of the *Journal of Policy Reform*, and he has written extensively on the theory and practice of trade policy. Currently he is a consultant to the World Bank and the Asian Development Bank.

GARY R. SAXONHOUSE is professor of economics at the University of Michigan and director of its Committee on Comparative and Historical Research on Market Economies. His work has ranged from studies on the structure and operation of the Japanese economy to analyses of technology transfer and econometrics. In 1995–1996 he was a fellow at the Center for Advanced Study in the Behavioral Sciences at Stanford University.

PAUL WONNACOTT is Alan R. Holmes Professor of Economics at Middlebury College and former member of the Council of Economic Advisers. He has written several books and published numerous journal articles on trade and economics, including most recently "Merchandise Trade in the Pacific Basin," in *The World Economy* (1995).

Preface

Free Trade Areas (FTA) have rapidly proliferated since the early 1980s, and U.S. trade policy now embraces them energetically. This is evident from the current administration's (and indeed the Bush administration's) desire to extend NAFTA to Chile and beyond, and from the occasional high-level expressions of interest in turning APEC into yet another FTA.[1]

Despite the popular equation of FTAs with genuine free trade, these are *preferential* trading arrangements, PTAs. They are therefore two-faced: they offer free trade to members but (implicitly) protection against nonmembers. Their economics is therefore far more complex than that of genuinely nondiscriminatory free trade. Indeed, the economics of PTAs makes them open to serious reservations, bringing into doubt the wisdom of the changed U.S. policy.

This volume advances new theoretical research that reminds us of this lesson, first taught in a seminal work on the subject by the great economist Jacob Viner in 1950. This research is contained in the substantial introductory chapter by the editors, synthesizing and extending the theory of PTAs that has emerged since Viner's work. The essay evaluates critically with this analysis the claims on behalf of PTAs that have been made by U.S. policy makers, in the Congress and in the administration, and by their economist allies in think tanks and, also, in universities. The essay concludes that the change in U.S. policy, encouraging PTAs instead of frowning on them in favor of single-minded pursuit of multilateral nonpreferential trade liberalization, has been a mistake.

A short summary of the reasons for this conclusion follows below.

---

1. Indeed, it is generally believed that the U.S. representative on the Eminent Persons Group, which was appointed by the member governments of APEC and which provided intellectual input into the process, was in favor of such a transformation of APEC until the Asian members firmly declined to sacrifice MFN by forming an FTA under GATT Article XXIV or (as astonishingly suggested by some) by undertaking partial trade barrier reductions only for APEC members by getting a waiver to Article XXIV.

It ties in also the remaining chapters in this volume that address the rise of regionalism in U.S. trade policy, and specifically the progress and problems with NAFTA and APEC, which (outside of the historic European Community initiated by the Treaty of Rome in 1957) remain the principal recent largescale PTAs or efforts to create one.

Exploding Some Popular Claims Favoring PTAs

In particular, we analyze and reject in chapter 1 several popular arguments recently advanced in favor of PTAs. Among them, we highlight the following:

Claim 1. PTAs between "natural trading partners" are desirable: the naturalness being defined typically as large initial trade volume shares with member countries, or a smaller distance between them, vis-à-vis nonmember countries.

It is argued that PTAs between such "natural trading partners" will produce less of the damaging "trade diversion" that can attend PTAs.[2] But, as we show, such an argument is a fallacy. Consider only three main arguments from our essay.

First, at best, it is a confusion between a smaller *scope* for trade diversion and a larger *outcome* of it. At worst, it confuses the *average* with the *margin* (which is a typical confusion in popular writings). These confusions are underscored by us with analytical arguments within well-defined and realistic models in the essay.

Second, our analysis demonstrates that higher trade volumes at the creation of a PTA can lead to greater, not smaller, losses to a member country that comes to the PTA from a higher initial set of tariffs, since that will redistribute tariff revenues away from it to the other members with lower initial tariffs. This is a point of relevance, for instance, when high-tariff poor countries join a PTA with low-tariff, hegemonic entities (such as the United States or the European Union), as with Mexico and the United States in NAFTA.

Third, the "natural" high volume of trade occurring initially before a PTA is formed with another country may itself be the "artificial" result of earlier preferences, as with U.S.-Canada free trade in autos and the offshore assembly in the *maquiladoras* in Mexico. In that case, new preferences are effectively sought to be justified by reference to old preferences! Again, we construct an analytical example that shows that such argument, while ludicrous on the face of it, is also dangerous.

---

2. Trade diversion occurs when trade is switched from efficient nonmember suppliers to inefficient member suppliers. The reason for this is that the members enter PTA markets duty free, while the nonmembers do not.

Added preferences, on top of earlier preferences and induced higher intermember trade volumes, can result in welfare losses to a member country.[3]

Claim 2. Based on Claim 1, PTAs that are "regional"—that is, have members who are contiguous or share common borders—must also be beneficial.

Of course, Claim 1 itself is untenable, as we have just seen. But even the notion that "regional" PTAs must have larger trade volumes with one another is not valid—despite claims made to the contrary by Summers and Krugman and denied by Bhagwati.

Our chapter notes that the support which Jeffrey Frenkel et al. have claimed to provide recently for Claim 2, through the use of gravity models that show bilateral distance to be an explanatory factor in explaining bilateral trade volumes, is a non sequitur. What is at issue is not distance as an explanatory factor; it is whether distance between every pair of trading countries correlates with their pairwise trade volumes. And it quite obviously does not. Besides, Jacques Polak has recently pointed out that even the gravity model does not work once distance is properly allowed for by using a location index that reflects the true distance of a country in trade: once such an index is used, the Frenkel demonstration of distance as an explanatory factor loses significance for recent years.[4]

And then we also must note that using notions such as regionalism to include members with large initial volumes of trade with one another runs into obvious difficulties in practice. South Korea may

3. This example is based on a classic model of the Nobel laureate James Meade who, we believe, was a multilateral free trader like most of the great international economists of his generation, including Gottfried Haberler and Jacob Viner. In fact, the focus of his trade-and-welfare analysis was always cosmopolitan, or what we call *world*, welfare, whether he was analyzing free trade or Free Trade Areas. This is what crucially sets apart his early contribution to the theory of domestic distortions from the revolution in the theory of commercial policy set off later by Bhagwati and Ramaswami. Their focus was on optimal and next-best interventions when the objective is *national* welfare. Their central insight, which greatly strengthened the case for free trade as a desirable trade policy for a nation, is that the scope for protection as the optimal policy is restricted to a narrow class of market failures where the distortions are external rather than domestic.

4. See his forthcoming article in *The World Economy*. The reader may best understand Polak's basic point by noting that it matters whether New Zealand and Australia are far out from the world economy and trading mainly with each other or whether they are positioned close to the European Union or North America.

have a large volume of trade with the United States, and so may Chile; but the two have little trade with each other. So, is putting all three into a "regional" arrangement within, say, APEC as a PTA going to be welfare-improving? Such internal "intransitivities" or contradictions are inevitable, rendering the notion of regionalism in Claim 2 almost laughable in practice, amenable to political posturing rather than reflecting economic soundness.

Claim 3. Since PTAs are formed under GATT Article XXIV auspices, its provisions enjoining that the average external tariff of the PTA not rise should shield nonmembers against losses imposed by trade diversion.

But, even disregarding the fact that an unchanged, weighted average of external tariffs is no guarantor of unchanged effect on the welfare of nonmembers, the problem with this claim is that it simply does not come to grips with the fact that today's trade barriers come more in the form of administered protection: for example, as VERs and other export restraints imposed on the exporting countries and antidumping actions against their firms. These protectionist weapons have the inherent property that they are elastic (for example, the estimated antidumping margins and hence the tariffs justified therewith are subject to serious arbitrariness and manipulation within national administrative procedures) *and* selective (for example, the antidumping actions typically target not merely specific countries but specific firms within an industry, whereas VERs almost always target particular countries). The lack of effective discipline in these matters then enables member countries to discriminate effectively against nonmembers, making it possible and even likely that trade creation (which would materialize in the absence of induced trade barriers against nonmembers) will be converted into trade diversion by resorting to such discrimination against nonmembers at the margin. Evidence for this is available from recent experience, such as when Mexico, faced by the peso crisis under the Ernesto Zedillo administration, raised several tariffs whose incidence was principally on nonmembers while sparing its NAFTA partners.

The "Spaghetti Bowl" Effect. Whereas the claims in favor of PTAs are weak at best and specious and founded on unscientific assertions at worst, the principal reason to condemn the PTAs remains the classic argument for multilateralism: that it builds trade liberalization on the foundation of nondiscrimination.

In truth, the proliferation of PTAs, sanctioned under GATT Article XXIV (leave aside the lesser and hence generally yet more problematic preferential trade arrangements that have been permitted for developing countries under the so-called Enabling Clause and the explicit waivers to MFN obligation under Article I:1)[5] has led to a crisscrossing of trade preferences assigned to countries and hence to a veritable "spaghetti bowl," where products in most important markets today enjoy access on widely varying terms depending on where they are supposed to originate.[6] This has happened when in fact, owing to the globalization of production, the ability to say which product is which country's has become increasingly problematic and will get even more so.

In chapter 2 of this volume, Paul Wonnacott argues for hybrid FTA–customs union agreements in the future, to avoid the worst trade-impeding aspects of preferential trade agreements, and provides specific empirical support for our observation about the spaghetti bowl phenomenon that afflicts the world trading system today.

This is a nonsensical situation, with attendant transaction costs and opportunities to distort trade flows by administrative reclassification and facilitating corruption. It underlines the wisdom of an earlier generation in favor of MFN and its principle of nondiscrimination. In fact, with the generally benign intention of freeing trade, we have ironically reproduced the chaotic system of trade preferences that resulted from protectionist impulses in the 1930s!

Only Two Justifications for PTAs—And Neither Obtains Currently. Given this analysis, we argue that PTAs ought to be returned to the traditional disfavor accorded to them by the United States, except in either of two compelling circumstances:

- that a group of countries wishes to opt for truly deep integration, both economic and political, with dismantled barriers to capital and labor mobility and aiming at common political structures such as a parliament and even uniform foreign policies; this is the model uniquely of the core European Community with its Single Market
- that the road to multilateral dismantling of trade barriers using the multilateral trade negotiations (MTN) approach under GATT/WTO auspices is closed, and taking the Article XXIV route is then the only available route to further trade liberalization, as the United States found in November 1982 when Europe refused to start a new MTN and

---

5. See table A1–1 at the end of chapter 1 for details of the several preferential agreements approved at the GATT under these three alternative possibilities.

6. This argument has been developed more fully by Bhagwati in his contribution in chapter 1 in Jagdish Bhagwati and Anne Krueger, *The Dangerous Drift to Preferential Trade Agreements* (Washington, D.C., AEI Press, 1995).

the United States decided to go the Article XXIV road with Canada, following then with NAFTA

To persist, however, with the Article XXIV route, through further expansion of PTAs, when the MTN route was jump-started with the initiation of the Uruguay Round in 1986, and when the Round was completed subsequently and the GATT was transformed into the WTO, is to keep on the dirt path when the turnpike has opened up. We argue at length in chapter 1 that this is truly a mistake.[7] Indeed, both the European Union and the United States, when seeking Free Trade Areas with other countries (as evident from table A1–1), are guilty of indulging this folly.

What to Do?

Our analysis then leads to two natural questions:

• Can we stop the drift toward ever more PTAs by illuminating, as in this essay, the critical distinctions between FTAs and free trade?
• If, with many politicians currently wedded to traveling the PTA route for several reasons, it is not possible to persuade most of them into giving up on them, how do we defang these PTAs so as to minimize the harm they bring?

The attempt to halt the drift to PTAs is not altogether a lost cause. Gary Saxonhouse, in chapter 3, clearly demonstrates the escape of APEC from the pressures of the United States to turn it into an Article XXIV style FTA, or at least into a non-MFN preferential trading area that would be granted a waiver from Article XXIV. In the end, the Asian members of APEC insisted on MFN trade liberalization, forcing the issue in favor of nonpreferential trade liberalization, in keeping with their traditional distaste for a preferential approach to the world's markets. Indeed, these Asian nations have clearly seen that the phrase "open regionalism" is deceptive when all it means is that new members may apply and be accepted if approved by national legislatures, with all the "nontrade" conditions that are now attached to such membership. True "open regionalism" on the trade front is in fact MFN liberalization, which openly and freely extends the trade barrier reductions to all.

Moreover, even NAFTA's expansion southwards, with Chile waiting in the wings, has currently been stalled: but the reason for that is

---

7. We discuss and dismiss the argument that going down the PTA route alongside the MTN route facilitates movement down the latter route.

not disenchantment with the PTA approach but rather divisions between the Democrats and the Republicans on the issue of the nontrade, labor, and environmental preconditions for such an extension. The former generally want tougher conditions, the latter generally want to delink trade from such preconditions.

In chapter 4, Claude Barfield analyses the factors behind the rise of regionalism in U.S. trade policy, as well as the unfortunate drift toward demands for ever stricter reciprocity in trade agreements. He argues that the debate over labor and environmental preconditions and over reciprocity (particularly in APEC) will increase in coming years, dividing proponents of a more liberal trade environment.

Despite the current puncturing of the PTA balloon in these ways, the threat from PTAs remains serious, warranting attention to ways of defanging them. Two ways of doing this can be distinguished.

One approach, to which many international economists have recently contributed, is to seek ways to strengthen Article XXIV to ensure that its discipline on member states is enhanced, and to ensure that nonmembers are not harmed and trade diversion is minimized. The problem with this approach, even though it has attracted ingenious proposals, is that few countries are now altogether without some PTA membership. Asking them to vote on making their life difficult is like asking criminals to decide on their own sentencing. One may therefore be cynical and expect little to come out of this approach.

Of course, recalling our earlier discussion, we should reiterate also the proposal, made by Bhagwati, that the growth of PTAs requires, to avoid trade diversion through the selective exercise of administered protection against nonmembers, that the disciplines on antidumping and VERs be greatly strengthened.

The other approach is to take the PTAs as, in effect, hard to shape and reshape: after all, it is of their very essence that they discriminate. So, noting that the preferences they give to members are relative to the trade barriers that are in place against nonmembers, we can work to eliminate them by seeking worldwide free trade at the border: preferences relative to zero are zero! For this reason, among others, a number of economists have proposed recently that the WTO adopt a target date, such as 2010, the way that PTAs have, for the completion of the worldwide freeing of trade.[8]

---

8. This proposal has occurred to many independently, whereas the chief and earliest proponent in print was Martin Wolf, the brilliant columnist for the *Financial Times*. It has been endorsed by leading policy makers since Wolf's advocacy in his newspaper, among them Donald Johnston, Secretary General of the OECD. Renato Ruggiero, Director General of the WTO, has also ex-

In the end, the main contribution of the present volume is to alert the policy makers to the substantial shift that is occurring in scholarly circles with regard to the wisdom of pursuing PTAs, to demonstrate that many of the pro-PTA arguments in the public domain are shallow, and to suggest an agenda for world trade liberalization that returns it to its earlier focus on multilateral, MFN, and MTN principles. We hope that we have met with a measure of success.

The essays in this volume were presented originally at a conference organized jointly by the American Enterprise Institute, Washington, D.C., and the Center for International Economics at the University of Maryland at College Park on June 12–13, 1996. We are grateful to Claude Barfield, Director, Trade Policy Studies, AEI, and Guillermo Calvo, Director, CIE, for making the conference possible.

---

pressed interest in it. Several economists from around the world also endorsed it in a letter to the editor in the *Financial Times* on June 25, 1996, developing the rationale for such a target more fully.

1
Preferential Trading Areas and Multilateralism—Strangers, Friends, or Foes?

Jagdish Bhagwati and Arvind Panagariya

The question of Preferential Trading Areas, as we should call them in preference to Free Trade Areas and customs unions, phrases that falsely equate them in the public mind and discourse with nonpreferential free trade, has not been distant from international economists' thoughts and concerns since the beginning of the postwar period when the architects of the General Agreement on Tariffs and Trade had to confront PTAs and accommodate them into the GATT via Article XXIV.[1]

Their wisdom became a center of analytical attention, especially at the time of the steps taken to form the European Community by the Treaty of Rome in 1957 and when, in what Bhagwati (1991) has called

We thank Jeffrey Frankel, Philip Levy, T.N. Srinivasan, Robert Staiger, and participants in the CIE-AEI Conference in June 1995, as well as Pravin Krishna, for many helpful conversations and comments on an earlier draft. We have also benefited from suggestions made at seminars at Harvard and Osaka universities, the University of Maryland, and the Stockholm School of Economics. Special appreciation is expressed to Maria Pillinini of the Development Division of the World Trade Organization for providing the list of PTAs at the end of this chapter in appendix table 1A–1.

1. The focus of our chapter will be on Article XXIV-sanctioned PTAs, rather than on every kind of preferential arrangement among any subset of World Trade Organization (WTO) members. PTAs, often grouped together into a single category, actually fall into three different WTO categories: Article XXIV arrangements involving FTAs and CUs, Enabling Clause arrangements limited to developing countries and permitting partial preferences, and Generalized System of Preferences (GSP) arrangements permitted via a grant of an exception to Article I. Appendix table 1A–1 provides a complete list of PTAs reported to WTO to date according to the WTO category within which they fall.

the period of First Regionalism, other Article XXIV-sanctioned PTAs were considered and even attempted in other areas.[2] The theory of PTAs of Viner (1950)—to which Meade (1955), Lipsey (1957, 1960), and other international economists at the time made important contributions—while preceding the formation of the European Community, developed more fully as a result of that singular event. The attempts at providing a more realistic rationale for the extension of such PTAs to developing countries, on the other hand, as a way of reducing the cost of any targeted level of industrialization, came from Cooper and Massell (1965a, 1965b), Johnson (1965), and Bhagwati (1968) at the time.[3]

It must be said that the First Regionalism was stillborn; beyond the European Community (and its offshoot, the European Free Trade Association), there was practically no successful emulation of the European developments elsewhere. At the same time, given the fact that it arose over the concerns that such PTAs were not the same as nondiscriminatory freeing of trade, the Vinerian theory was "static," concerning itself simply with the issue as to when such PTAs would be trade-diverting or trade-creating, thus diminishing or increasing welfare.

The recent revival of interest in the theory of Preferential Trading Areas, marking what Bhagwati (1991) has christened the Second Regionalism, has come instead from the conversion of the United States to preferential trading arrangements, starting with the Canada-U.S. Free Trade Agreement (CUFTA) and the later extension to include Mexico under the North American Free Trade Agreement (NAFTA). This time around, the movement has extended equally to other areas, involving again developing countries on their own, as in the Southern Cone Common Market (MERCOSUR), but with success rather than failure.

In 1982, the United States could not get multilateral trade talks started at Geneva and hence turned to ever-expanding PTAs as an alternative way of getting eventually to worldwide free trade. This has given the theory of PTAs a "dynamic time-path" dimension (Bhagwati

---

2. The reasons why these did not succeed are discussed in Bhagwati (1991).

3. These different approaches, and the later approaches to the static theory of preferential trading areas by Kemp and Wan (1976) and Brecher and Bhagwati (1981), have been distinguished and discussed in the graduate textbook by Bhagwati and Srinivasan (1983). The Cooper-Massell-Johnson-Bhagwati argument has also been formalized recently, using the Kemp-Wan approach and combining it with the theory of noneconomic objectives, by Krishna and Bhagwati (1994).

1993a). When would such an approach lead to a progressive freeing of trade barriers through expanding membership (and/or accelerating multilateral trade negotiations in a benign symbiosis)? This is also a political economy–theoretic question, fitting nicely into the modern preoccupation of economic theorists with questions relating to what policies emerge (that is, with "public choice") rather than what they should be (that is, with "social choice").

From a policy viewpoint also, this revival of PTAs is an important development. It was fed (if not led) by the U.S.-centered NAFTA and its proposed extension to Chile and beyond, and by Asia-Pacific Economic Cooperation (APEC), which some in the United States would like to see turn into another PTA, and by the call of European politicians such as Foreign Minister Klaus Kinkel of Germany at the outset, and by many others subsequently, to form TAFTA (a Transatlantic Free Trade Area). With WTO jumpstarted and multilateralism functioning, the theoretical and policy questions then must be confronted: should these proposals for proliferating PTAs, especially when inclusive of hegemonic powers such as the United States, be encouraged by economists?

In this chapter we undertake the following tasks. After reviewing key phrases and concepts, we extend the "static" analysis of PTAs. This enables us to examine several recent claims in favor of PTAs and persuades us to discard them as unpersuasive.

Specifically, our analysis enables us to examine and reject the much-cited claim that it is wrong to worry about trade diversion and that PTAs are generally as good as nonpreferential trade liberalization.

Our analysis gives added insight into why the usual argument made these days is mistaken. This is the argument that when countries joining a PTA have large shares of their trade with one another and are thus "natural trading partners," they need not fear losses. The non-hegemonic countries that are liberalizing with a hegemon that is generally open and offering few new reductions of trade barriers, as is the case with Mexico and with other potential NAFTA members outside of the United States and Canada, could face the prospect of significant "static" welfare losses.

Next, we turn to the dynamic time-path question. In the policy context, this necessitates our considering arguments as to why a proliferation of PTAs, despite their creating a harmful "spaghetti-bowl" phenomenon in the world economy, may be beneficial because of their helpful consequences for the progressive freeing of trade and moving the world economy to worldwide free trade.

We systematize the current analytical contributions on this problem and evaluate the current policy developments.[4] It is our view that PTAs that are hegemon centered, as NAFTA is, are not the desirable way to advance the cause of worldwide freeing of trade barriers and that it is better to focus on WTO-centered MFN trade liberalization. By contrast, we consider intradeveloping-country, non-hegemon-centered PTAs, such as MERCOSUR, in a more favorable light. First, however, we need to clarify a few central phrases and concepts.

Phrases and Concepts

Two phrases are frequently used: PTAs and regionalism. The two significant concepts are, first, trade creation and diversion and, second, stumbling and building blocks.

Preferential Trading Areas. This term refer to FTAs, CUs (which also have a common external tariff), and Common Markets (which additionally have freedom of internal factor movement within the area defined by member states). All these arrangements fall within the purview of GATT Article XXIV. Lesser forms have traditionally been permitted for developing countries and come under Economic Cooperation among Developing Countries (ECDC). We will have something to say about that too, though our chapter will be almost exclusively focused on Article XXIV-sanctioned PTAs and, within that category, on FTAs in particular.

Regionalism. This term has been loosely used by many, including us, as synonymous with PTAs. Strictly speaking, however, regionalism refers to PTAs defined by a geographic region. There is a school of thought (to which Lawrence Summers and Paul Krugman have subscribed) that considers regional PTAs to be a priori less likely to lead to static trade diversion than nonregional PTAs and such regional PTAs to be therefore ipso facto acceptable. This is a substantive issue that we will consider, as did Bhagwati (1993a) in a preliminary way. Our focus, however, will be on PTAs, not regional PTAs.

Trade Creation and Trade Diversion (Viner). The concepts of trade creation and trade diversion as two possibilities that define the second-best nature of the static analysis of PTAs go back to Viner (1950), of course. While there are various ways in which these two concepts have

---

4. Our analytical synthesis draws on Bhagwati, Krishna, and Panagariya (1996) and also on our paper for the 1996 American Economic Association meetings in San Francisco, Bhagwati and Panagariya (1996).

subsequently been defined, we will use them (in the theoretical analysis below) in the original Vinerian sense to mean a shift of imports from an efficient to an inefficient source under trade diversion, and a shift from an inefficient to an efficient source under trade creation.[5]

"Stumbling Blocks" and "Building Blocks" (Bhagwati). The phraseology and conceptualization of PTAs that, in a dynamic time-path sense, contribute to the multilateral freeing of trade either by progressively adding new members (down the PTA path to worldwide free trade) or by prompting accelerated multilateral trade negotiations and are thus *building blocks* toward the multilateral freeing of trade and those that do the opposite and hence are *stumbling blocks* to the goal of worldwide, multilateral freeing of trade, owes to Bhagwati (1991, 77) and has been adopted by Lawrence (1991) and others.[6] Insofar as Viner's trade creation and trade diversion concepts were designed to divide PTAs into those that were good and those that were bad in the static sense, Bhagwati's building block and stumbling block concepts are designed to divide PTAs into those that are good and those that are bad in the dynamic, time-path sense.

Rethinking Static Welfare Analysis

We now begin with the static analysis. Frankly, so much has been written on the static analysis since Viner's pioneering 1950 contribution, indeed by virtually every important international economist, that one may think that there is little to add.

The Issues Examined. Yet there is something to be gained by another, close look at the conventional static analysis in view of several presup-

---

5. In Viner's analysis, reproduced in figure 1-1, with constant costs everywhere, the concepts translate immediately into a shift of imports from the outside to the partner country as trade diversion and a shift from the home country production to imports from the partner country as trade creation. This translation does not hold fully in figure 1-3, for example.

6. In a generous introductory footnote to his article entitled "Emerging Regional Arrangements: Building Blocks or Stumbling Blocks?" Lawrence (1991) writes, "I owe this phrase to Jagdish Bhagwati." Bhagwati (1991, 77) refers to the expansion of membership as a test of PTAs serving as "building blocks" for worldwide freeing of trade: this concept is illustrated in figure 1-9, reproduced from Bhagwati (1993a). Evidently, if going down the PTA path can trigger multilateral negotiations and their successful conclusion, that too can be a way in which PTAs may serve as building blocks, as discussed here.

5

positions, mostly favorable to PTAs, which have recently been made by policy analysts.

It has been forcefully argued by Summers (1991, 299) in an influential paper that international economists should not be preoccupied by trade diversion: "I find it surprising that this issue is taken so seriously—in most other situations, economists laugh off second best considerations and focus on direct impacts."

Our first reaction is to deny the premise of his analogy: economists, faced with a second-best problem, typically *do* worry about that aspect of the problem. Indeed, if the world was first best, market prices would reflect social opportunity costs, and there would be no need for cost-benefit analysis for projects. The World Bank, where Summers served with distinction, would then have to close down most of its project-lending research and analysis aimed at determining the shadow prices to be used in judging the acceptability of projects.

Second, the problem of preferential trade liberalization is indeed an inherently second-best problem since nondiscriminatory trade liberalization is being ruled out. Ignoring this aspect is unwarranted.

Third, one should not confuse "second best" with "primary impact." First-best problems also are characterized by primary and total effects.

Fourth, if Summers implies that trade-diverting PTAs are a minor nuisance, he is misled presumably by the fact that efficiency losses are Harberger triangles and "small." But such PTAs impose losses on member countries also through tariff-revenue-*redistribution*, and these can be large: they are rectangles, while the efficiency effects are triangles.

We also consider the contention in the recent policy debate that countries that trade with each other in larger volume than with other nations are "natural" trading partners and hence that PTAs among them are likely to be welfare enhancing to their members for that reason.

This contention is further linked with the argument that "regional" PTAs are desirable (in the sense of being more likely to create welfare gains for their members) because geographically contiguous countries (particularly if they share common borders) have larger volumes of trade with one another than with others.

Our analysis here challenges the premise that large volumes of initial trade lessen the likelihood of loss from PTAs. Consequently, it also undermines the associated contention that regional PTAs are more desirable.

We also question the alternative but related "natural trading partners" hypothesis that regional PTAs are likely to improve welfare by conserving on transport costs. We show that transport costs by themselves do not provide a reason for discriminatory PTAs.[7]

The Theoretical Analysis. Since Viner's classic work in 1950, PTAs have been considered to be harmful both to member countries (whose imports are the subject of the trade diversion) and to the world when trade diversion arises, and to be welfare enhancing when trade creation occurs instead. This ambiguity of outcomes, depending on the relative strengths of the two effects when a PTA is formed, has been the principal reason for the debate among economists as to whether a specific PTA is desirable.

We will begin the theoretical analysis below by showing, however, that the conventional trade creation and trade diversion are not the entire story in deciding on the welfare outcome for an *individual* member of a PTA. Even if trade creation effects are larger than trade diversion effects so that the union as a whole benefits, an individual member could lose on account of adverse income distribution effects arising from tariff revenue redistribution.

The redistribution of tariff revenue between member countries arises, of course, from a shift in the terms of trade within the union. When a member country lowers its tariff on the partner without lowering it on the rest of the world, within-union terms of trade shift in favor of the partner (for both existing and new imports from it). The extent of the unfavorable redistributive effect on a member country is obviously determined by the degree of preferential access it gives to the partner country in relation to the preferential access it receives from the latter: the greater the margin of preference the country gives, the more it stands to lose. This implies that when a country with a high degree of protection forms a PTA with a country with relatively open markets, as is the case of Mexico and the United States, the former may well be faced with a net welfare loss. We develop this theme and its ramifications, in the following analysis, using simple models from the literature and distinguishing clearly among the effects on member country and world welfare.

---

7. The "natural trading partners" hypothesis comes therefore in two forms. In the first form, the emphasis is on a large initial volume of trade that may result, *inter alia*, from geographical proximity. In the second form, the emphasis is on transport costs that are assumed to be low between countries within the same region. We have been firmly informed by Paul Wonnacott that the term "natural trading partner" originated in Wonnacott and Lutz (1989). Many authors have attributed the term instead to Krugman (1991a), who, along with Summers, should nevertheless be credited with popularizing it.

The Viner Model—Constant Costs. The natural starting point for explaining the economics of regional integration is Viner's partial equilibrium model. This model does not fully capture the effects noted above but is, nevertheless, an important step toward understanding them. Assume that there are three countries, A, B, and C. Countries A and B are potential union partners and C represents the rest of the world. In figure 1-1, panels a and b, let $M_A M_A$ represent A's import demand for a specific product and $P_B E_B$ and $P_C E_C$ the (export) supplies of the same product available from B and C, respectively. Following Viner, it is assumed that the supply prices of B and C are constant at P_B and P_C, respectively. In panel a, the supply price of C exceeds that of B and in panel b the opposite is true.

In panel a illustrating the case of a *trade-creating union*, with an initial nondiscriminatory specific tariff t, A imports OM_0 quantity of the good.[8] All imports come from B so that A raises areas 1 and 2 in tariff revenue. If A now forms an FTA with B, imports from B expand from OM_0 to OM_{FTA}. The tariff revenue disappears, but the price facing consumers declines by t; A's consumers capture the entire revenue in the form of increased surplus. Because B is the lower cost source of the product, there is positive trade creation and no trade diversion.[9] Working like nondiscriminatory free trade, the FTA yields to A and to the union a net gain represented by areas 3 and 4.[10]

Panel b illustrates the case of a *trade-diverting union*. Here B is the higher cost source of the product with the result that, given a nondiscriminatory tariff in A, all imports come from C. A imports OM_0 and collects areas 1 and 2 in tariff revenue. If A and B now form an FTA, imports expand to OM_{FTA}, but the source of their supply switches from C to B. Though the reduction in A's domestic price leads to some trade creation—increased imports lead to a displacement of some inefficient domestic production and increase in consumption in A—the switch to the higher cost source, B, leads to a large trade diversion of OM_0 quantity of imports from C to B. Thus, panel b shows a case where the union diverts trade from C, but it also creates some trade. The gains to A are given by area 3 and the losses by area 2. The loss of area 2 results from a deterioration in A's terms of trade from P_C to P_B and takes the form

---

8. We assume a specific rather than an ad valorem tariff for geometric simplicity when supply curves are rising. Nothing in the analysis hangs on it.

9. Because imports expand, some of the inefficient domestic production is replaced by imports from B. A also gains from an increase in the consumers' surplus in excess of the tariff revenue.

10. B gains nothing and C loses nothing, given the constant-cost assumptions on their supply curves in trade.

of the excess of the loss of tariff revenue $(1 + 2)$ over that which is captured partially (1) by A's consumers. Area 2 goes to pay for the higher cost of production in B than in C.

Now, unless cost differences between B and C are small, areas similar to area 2 will be large in relation to the triangular areas of gain. The welfare loss to A from the loss of revenue on diverted imports applies to the *entire* initial quantity of imports, whereas the gain applies only to the *change* in the quantity of imports. The FTA will be associated with trade creation in some sectors and trade diversion in others. But since losses are likely to be large in cases involving trade diversion, trade diversion in even a few sectors can more than offset the gains arising from trade creation in a large number of sectors.

The trade-diverting case of panel b can also be illustrated in general equilibrium by using the Lipsey (1958) version of the Viner analysis as in panel c. There, the economy of A is specialized in producing at $\bar{Y}$, with $\bar{Y}C$ and $\bar{Y}B$ the given, fixed terms of trade with C and B, respectively. With an initial nondiscriminating tariff, A trades with C and consumes at C^{IS}, winding up with welfare at $U_C{}^A$. With the FTA between A and B, the trade shifts to B. A winds up consuming at C^{FTA} and its welfare is reduced to $U_B{}^A$. The welfare loss QN can then be seen as the difference between the tariff-revenue or terms-of-trade loss MN and the gain MQ that comes from the ability to shift consumption from $\hat{C}$ to C^{FTA}.[11] (OM is the income at domestic prices in the initial situation, and tariff revenue is MN, the sum of the two yielding ON as national expenditure.)

A final and obvious point may be stressed concerning nondiscriminatory trade liberalization by country A. In both the cases shown in figure 1–1, A obtains maximum trade gains and its welfare is improved relative to the initial as well as the FTA equilibrium by a nondiscriminatory liberalization. Such liberalization leads to the same equilibrium in the trade-creating union in panel a (as a limiting case) and eliminates trade diversion in the case in panel b, amounting to free trade with the most efficient supplier for each commodity.

Partner Country's Supply Curve Is Upward Sloped. Because of the assumption that the export-supply curves of both B and C are perfectly elastic, the model in figure 1–1 leads to at least two unrealistic out-

---

11. The measure used is the conventional Hicksian equivalent variation: keeping the initial nondiscriminatory tariff, how much income can A withdraw to yield the same welfare loss as the FTA imposes?

FIGURE 1–1
CONSTANT COSTS, ACCORDING TO STRICTLY VINERIAN ANALYSIS

Panel A. Trade-creating Union of A and B

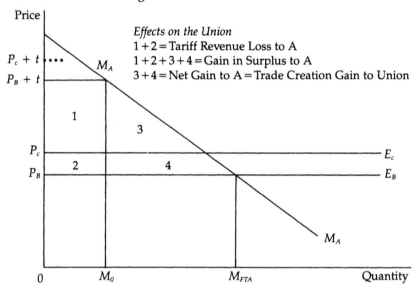

Panel B. Trade-Diverting Union of A and B

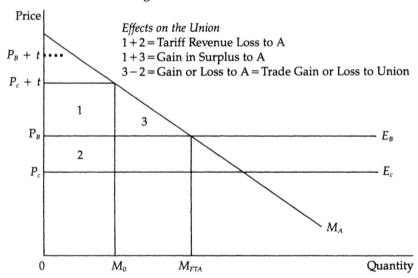

FIGURE 1–1 (continued)

Panel C. General Equilibrium Analysis: Viner-Lipsey Model of Trade-Diverting Union

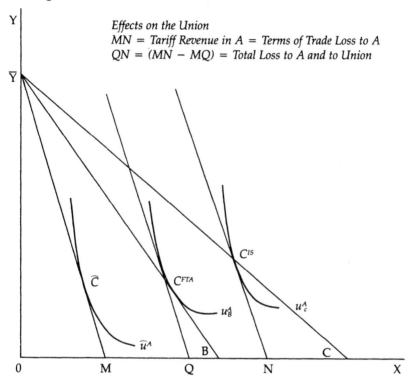

Effects on the Union
MN = Tariff Revenue in A = Terms of Trade Loss to A
QN = (MN − MQ) = Total Loss to A and to Union

comes.[12] First, imports into A come from either B or C but not both. Second, in the trade diversion case, the losses of A represented by area 2 are used up entirely to finance B's higher costs of production: the partner country B makes no gain whatsoever. The model thus captures only one side of the possibly "mercantilist" nature of trade-diverting FTAs: country A can lose from its own (discriminatory) trade liberalization, but country B does not gain from it.

A more realistic model allows the supply curve of one or both countries B and C to slope upward. In the interest of simplicity, we will allow for an upward-sloped supply curve for only one country at a time. Figure 1–2 takes up the case when the partner country B's supply curve slopes upward and that of the outside country C is horizontal. This case captures the essence of the more general model in which the outside country's supply curve also slopes upward but is more elastic than the partner's. Figure 1–3 shows instead the case when the union is between A and C so that the partner country's supply curve is more elastic than that of the outside world.

In both figures 1–2 and 1–3, as before, we then let $M_A M_A$ represent the import demand for a product imported by A. The supply curve of the product available from B is upward sloped and is represented by $E_B E_B$. Country C's export supply curve, represented by $P_C E_C$, is horizontal. The tariff continues to be specific. Consider then figure 1–2 and three cases: an initial nondiscriminatory tariff, free trade, and an FTA.

Under a *nondiscriminatory tariff* at rate t per unit, supplies from B and C, as perceived by buyers in A, are given by $E_B^t E_B^t$ and $P_C^t E_C^t$, respectively. Total imports into A equal OQ_3 of which OQ_1 come from B and $Q_1 Q_3$ from C. Country A collects tariff revenue equivalent to rectangle GHNS. The gains from trade for A amount to the area under the import-demand curve and above the domestic price plus the tariff revenue, that is, triangle KSG plus rectangle GHNS. For country B, the gains from trade equal the area above $E_B E_B$ and below the net price received, P_C, that is, area HUD. Country C neither gains nor loses from trade. Table 1–1 summarizes this information in column 1.

---

12. Many of the points in this and the following section have been made earlier in Panagariya (1995a, 1995b). The tariff-revenue-transfer effect central to our analysis is normally present in all models characterized by flexible terms of trade. Thus, see the three-good, three-country general-equilibrium analyses of Berglas (1979) and Riezman (1979), which are neatly summarized within a unified framework by Lloyd (1982). Both Berglas and Riezman find, as we do, that when intra-union terms of trade are flexible, a large volume of imports from the partner country is inversely related to the welfare effect of a preferential liberalization. Neither of these authors makes many of the points we make or looks at the problem as we do, however.

FIGURE 1–2

EFFECT OF UNION (A + B) WITH RISING COSTS FROM PARTNER COUNTRY

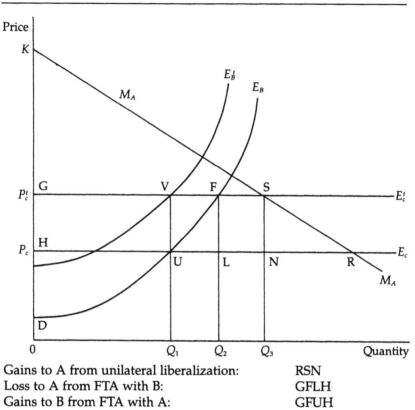

Gains to A from unilateral liberalization:	RSN
Loss to A from FTA with B:	GFLH
Gains to B from FTA with A:	GFUH
Net Loss from FTA:	FLU

Suppose instead that A decides to adopt a policy of *free trade* by eliminating the tariff on a nondiscriminatory basis. The price in A declines to P_C, imports from B do not change, and imports from C rise by NR. Tariff revenue disappears, but the gains from trade rise to KGS + GHNS + RSN: there is a net welfare gain to A of RSN. The extra gain comes from increased benefits to consumers and producers in A. The gains to country B remain unchanged at HDU. Because of the perfectly elastic supply, country C neither gains nor loses from trade before or after trade liberalization by A. Therefore, the world as a whole benefits by area RSN. These changes are summarized in column 2 of table 1–1.

Next, assume that A forms an FTA with B by eliminating entirely the tariff on B but retaining it on C. Imports from B rise to OQ_2, and

13

FIGURE 1–3

EFFECT OF UNION (A + C) WITH RISING COSTS FROM OUTSIDE COUNTRY

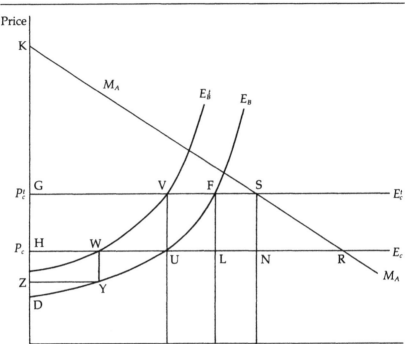

those from C decline to Q_2Q_3. Now B gains from the FTA due to an improvement in its terms of trade. The net price received by the exporters of B increases from P_C to $P_C{}^t$, and the gains from trade to B rise to HDU + GFUH. Country B gains from A's liberalization.

Because imports continue to come from C before as well as after the FTA and C's supply is perfectly elastic, the price in A is unchanged. But now that there is no tariff revenue on goods coming from B, A's gains from trade decline by GFLH. Stated differently, A's within-union terms of trade worsen by the full amount of the tariff liberalization: country A loses from its own liberalization. Because the FTA diverts imports Q_1Q_2 from the more efficient C to the less efficient B, A's loss exceeds B's gain by the area FLU. The world as a whole loses by the same area FLU. The last column in table 1–1 shows these changes.

It is now evident that Summers' earlier-cited argument that international economists should embrace PTAs because second-best "trade

TABLE 1-1
GAINS FROM TRADE UNDER UNILATERAL LIBERALIZATION AND FREE TRADE AREA
(COUNTRY A PLUS COUNTRY B)

Country	Nondiscriminatory Tariff (Initial Situation) (1)	Free Trade (FT) (2)	Free Trade Area (A and B) (FTA) (3)
A	KGS + GHNS	KGS + GHNS + RSN (A gains)	KGS + GHNS − GFLH (A loses)
B	HDU	HDU (no change)	HDU + (GFLH − FLU=) GFUH (B gains)
C	0	0 (no change)	0 (no change)
World	KGS + GHNS + HDU	KGS + GHNS + HDU + RSN (World gains)	KGS + GHNS + HDU − FLU (World loses)

NOTE: This table relates to figure 1-2 in the text. (1) World Welfare Loss from FTA compared with FT: FLU + RSN. (2) World Welfare Loss from FTA compared with Initial Situation: FLU.

15

diversion" worries are "laughable," and that primary effects must be considered to be dominant, is misplaced when impacts on the welfare of specific countries are considered. The loss to A from its own preferential liberalization arises primarily from the primary effect of the FTA. If we assume that the initial imports from the union partner are large, the loss to A in this wholly trade-diverting union is substantial.[13] It reflects the tariff revenues lost on the original imports (plus the new diverted imports) from the partner country B.

Clearly, FTAs can give rise to large redistributive effects (on original imports) between countries. The amount of trade diverted ($Q_1 Q_2$) may be small, and the loss to the union from this trade diversion is small because it is a triangle, but all this really has no relevance to our critique of Summers as just concluded.

Next, our analysis casts doubt on the recent presumption that countries that trade with each other in large volume are "natural" trading partners and regional arrangements among them must therefore be beneficial to them. It is not entirely clear from the literature what it means to be "natural" trading partners.[14] A quotation from Summers (1991, 297), however, should help:

> Are trading blocs likely to divert large amounts of trade? In answering this question, the issue of natural trading blocs is crucial because to the extent that blocs are created between countries that already trade disproportionately, the risk of large amounts of trade diversion is reduced.[15]

Later we consider this entire question of natural trading partners and their desirability. But our analysis so far already provides a devastating critique of the presumption advanced in favor of such natural trading blocs. It is evident from figure 1–2 that the larger the initial quantity of imports from a trading partner, the greater (not smaller) the loss to the country liberalizing preferentially, *ceteris paribus*. That is to say, the more natural the trading partner according to Summers's definition, the larger the loss from a discriminatory trade liberalization with it!

---

13. There is no trade creation in the example as the FTA leaves the domestic price and therefore total imports into A unchanged.

14. We discuss the natural trading partners hypothesis in the alternative context of transport costs later in the chapter.

15. In a similar vein, Krugman (1991a, 21) notes, "To reemphasize why this matters: if a disproportionate share of world trade would take place within trading blocs even in the absence of any preferential trading arrangement, then the gains from trade creation within blocs are likely to outweigh any possible losses from external trade diversion."

Finally, it has been frequently argued that, given today's low levels of trade restrictions, preferential trading arrangements are unlikely to be harmful: trade creation effects should dominate the outcome, making PTAs as good as FT (free trade). But this argument, plausible as it sounds, is contradicted by our analysis. Thus in figure 1–2, if the initial nondiscriminatory tariff is sufficiently high, an FTA between A and B can eliminate C as a supplier of the product. In this case, the FTA lowers the internal price in A and gives rise to trade creation. Under some (admittedly strong) conditions, this trade creation can outweigh the tariff-revenue loss and may improve welfare. By contrast, if the initial tariff is low, the chances are poor that the formation of the FTA will eliminate imports from C and lower the internal price.

The Outside Country's Supply Curve Is Upward Sloped. The conclusion that A's preferential liberalization hurts itself and benefits its union partner has been derived under the assumption that the supply of B is less than perfectly elastic and that of C is perfectly elastic. In this setting, the union partner is a less efficient supplier of the product than is the outside world. What will happen if the situation was reversed such that B's supply curve was perfectly elastic and C's less than perfectly elastic?

This case can be analyzed by letting A form a union with C rather than B. In this case, analyzed in figure 1–3, an FTA lowers the price in A to P_C. Though there is no gain to the union partner, A's gain from the FTA ($= RSN + HWYZ$) exceeds that under nondiscriminatory liberalization (that is, free trade) by the amount of tariff revenue ($= HWYZ$) collected on imports from the outside country.[16] This case brings us back to the conventional presumption that A's liberalization should benefit it (though the presumption that others should gain from the liberalization does not carry through for the outsider country B that loses). The precise welfare results, based on analysis of figure 1–3, are drawn together in table 1–2.

This case clearly undercuts the arguments about the dangers of PTAs to country A that were made in the previous section. Therefore, it is important to ask how relevant this case is empirically. It is perhaps reasonable to assert that a union partner is likely to resemble B in some products and C in other products, and therefore the effect of the FTA will be ambiguous in general.

A common claim has been that NAFTA is likely to benefit Mexico because the United States and Canada are very large and therefore the

16. *Ceteris paribus*, the less A trades with the outside country, the less tariff revenue it collects and the less is its gain. Thus, in the spirit of our previous discussion, a high proportion of trade with the partner implies smaller gains from preferential liberalization.

TABLE 1–2
GAINS FROM TRADE UNDER FREE TRADE AREA
(COUNTRY A PLUS COUNTRY C)

Country	Nondiscriminatory Tariff (1)	FTA (A and C) (2)
A	KGS + GHNS	KGS + GHNS + RSN + HWYZ (A gains)
B	HDU	ZYD = HDU − WYU − HWYZ (B loses)
C	0	0 (no change)
World	KGS + GHNS + HDU	KGS + GHNS + HDU + RSN − WYU (World may gain or lose according as RSN > < WYU)

NOTE: This table relates to figure 1–3 in the text. Column 1 is identical to Column (1) in table 1–1 and is reproduced here to facilitate comparison. The results under Free Trade are identical between the two FTAs, (A and B) and (A and C).

most efficient suppliers of a majority of Mexico's products. Our analysis suggests, however, at least two reasons why this conclusion is unwarranted.

First, given that the outside world includes the European Union, Japan, China, Korea, Hong Kong, and numerous other outward-oriented and highly competitive countries, the conclusion that the United States and Canada are the most efficient suppliers of a large majority of Mexico's products is highly suspect. Indeed, if it were true, we would be hard-pressed to explain the persistent demands for anti-dumping and other forms of protection in the United States.[17] Second, recall that if the union partner is a large supplier of imports, the tariff-redistribution losses to A in the case of trade diversion are large. Therefore, even if the union partner is the most efficient supplier of the majority of A's imports, losses may outweigh any gains. In the case of

17. In addition, a fraction of the large imports from the United States could well be a result of preferential policies rather than competitiveness.

NAFTA, the United States does account for a sufficiently large proportion of Mexico's imports for us to conjecture plausibly that the tariff-redistribution losses in trade-diversion cases could outweigh the gains in trade-creation cases.

This analysis has an important qualification that will be discussed in the next section. Before doing so, we mention two additional possibilities that are worthy of brief consideration: first, export-supply curves are upward sloped for both B and C; second, the products of A, B, and C are imperfect substitutes. In either of these cases, the small-country and small-union assumptions are violated, and a complete elimination of the tariff by A, whether on a discriminatory or nondiscriminatory basis, is not the optimal policy.[18] We will look at the second case in detail.

But here we note that our conclusions remain valid under the following circumstances. In case one, if the elasticity of supply of the outside country is high in relation to that of the union partner, B, a discriminatory tariff reduction is likely to hurt A itself while benefiting B. In case two, analyzed later in the chapter, if B's goods are poor substitutes for A's goods but not C's, as seems entirely plausible, discriminatory liberalization by A will hurt A itself and benefit the union partner, B, even at constant terms of trade, whereas the terms of trade effects will reinforce this outcome. Before we present this analysis in detail, an important qualification to figures 1–2 and 1–3 must be noted.

A Qualification and Modification. Figures 1–2 and 1–3 capture the essence of a large body of the literature on regional arrangements that emerged in the 1950s and 1960s. But these figures have an important limitation that has been ignored entirely in the literature until recently. They implicitly assume that either (1) the partner country maintains the same tariff as A on the product under consideration (that is, the arrangement is a Customs Union), or (2) the product is not consumed in the partner country. Let us explain why.

Consider first the case depicted in figure 1–2. The common practice in the literature, as in our foregoing analysis, has been to assume that post-FTA prices in a member country are determined by the price in the outside country, C, plus the country's own tariff. As Richardson (1994) has noted recently, however, this assumption is incorrect in general. It implies that, if tariffs in A and B are different, producer as well as consumer prices in A and B are different. But given duty-free move-

---

18. It is a common practice in the computable general-equilibrium (CGE) models to differentiate goods by the country of origin and yet impose the small-country assumption. To a general equilibrium theorist, this is not correct. If a country is the sole producer of its exports, it necessarily has market power.

ment of goods produced within the union, producer prices between A and B must equalize under an FTA.

Assume that the tariff on the product under consideration is lower in B than in A, violating condition one above. In figure 1–2, recall that $E_B E_B$ is B's supply curve for exports, that is, output supply net of domestic consumption. Under a nondiscriminatory tariff in A, B's producers sell OQ_1 in A. Because the net price received by exporters on sales in A is P_C, the domestic price in B will also be P_C. If A and B now form an FTA and the price in A remains $P_C{}^t$, producers in B have no incentive to sell anything in their domestic market unless the price there also rises to $P_C{}^t$. But given that the tariff in B is lower than that in A, the price in B cannot rise to $P_C{}^t$, and the entire quantity of the product previously sold in B is diverted to A. The rules of origin can forbid the diversion of goods *imported* from C to A but not of goods *produced* in B.[19] Unless domestic consumption of the product in B is zero (assumption two above), B's export-supply curve shifts to the right by the quantities demanded in B at each price, that is, B's export-supply curve coincides with its output-supply curve.

Figure 1–4 lays out how the allowance for the diversion of B's domestic sales to A after the formation of the FTA affects our conclusions. It reproduces figure 1–2, omitting $E_B{}'E_B{}'$. In the initial equilibrium, with a nondiscriminatory tariff in A, imports from B are OQ_1 as in figure 1–2. After the FTA is formed, the expansion of exports is larger than that given by point F. How much larger it is will depend on where B's total supply curve lies. There are three possibilities.[20]

First, if the total supply curve intersects $M_A M_A$ above point S as shown by $S_B S_B$, the results of the previous section hold with a vengeance.[21] Exports from B now expand more than in figure 1–2, and losses to A from the transfer of tariff revenue are larger. In this case, B's producers sell all of their output in A and receive the same price as A's producers, namely, $P_C{}^t$. The entire quantity consumed in B is imported from C, with consumers paying a price lower than $P_C{}^t$. Country A imports from countries B and C.

Second, suppose that B's supply curve intersects $M_A M_A$ between S and W, where the height of W is P_C plus the tariff in B. In this case, the price in A is determined by the height of the point of intersection of

---

19. Rules of origin can and do, of course, restrict trade in other ways. For a recent analysis of how rules of origin can lead to welfare-worsening outcomes, see Krueger (1993, 1995).

20. See Grossman and Helpman (1995) in this context.

21. Note that the horizontal difference between $E_B E_B$ and $S_B S_B$ declines as price rises. This is because the demand in B must fall with a rise in the price.

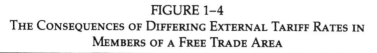

FIGURE 1–4

THE CONSEQUENCES OF DIFFERING EXTERNAL TARIFF RATES IN
MEMBERS OF A FREE TRADE AREA

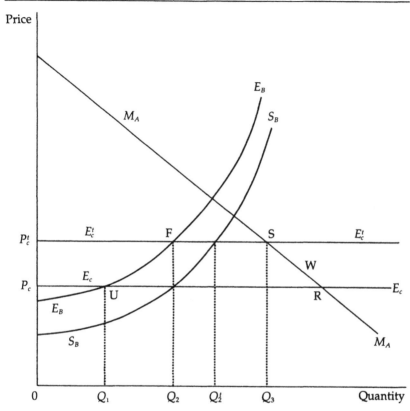

B's supply curve and $M_A M_A$. Because this price is below P_c^t, a part of
the lost tariff revenue is now captured by A's consumers. But we still
have a tariff-revenue transfer to firms in B. The transfer is larger the
closer the intersection point of the two curves to S. Producers in B sell
all their output in A, A does not import anything from C, and B imports everything from C.

Finally, if B's supply curve intersects $M_A M_A$ below point W, the
price in A drops to the tariff-inclusive price in B given by the height of
point W. All of A's imports come from B with producers in B selling in
A as well as B. Both consumer and producer prices equalize between
A and B. In this case, the redistributive effect is a declining function of
the tariff in B. In the limit, if the external tariff in B is zero, the FTA

leads to free trade in A (just as in B).

The case depicted in figure 1–3 is also modified along the lines of figure 1–4 if the good in question is consumed in the partner country (C) and the latter levies a tariff lower than that of A. To illustrate, assume that the tariff in C is zero, and the demand for the product in C at P^C is larger than B's supply at that price. Then, B can sell all it wants to export at P^C to C. In the post-FTA equilibrium, A's imports come entirely from C, while B sells all its exports to C. The tariff revenue raised by A on imports from B in figure 1–3 is no longer available, and A's gains from the FTA with C are reduced to triangle RSN, the same as under unilateral, nondiscriminatory liberalization.

An Imperfect-Substitutes Model. An unrealistic implication of the model just explored is that, under an FTA, either producers of B must sell all their output in A and none in their domestic market (the first two cases) or consumers in A must import everything from B and none from C (the last case). This conclusion does not require a complete FTA; it can hold true even in the presence of a small tariff preference as long as external tariffs in the two countries are different. A quick examination of the direction of trade data of member countries of preferential trading arrangements such as the Association of Southeast Asian Nations (ASEAN) and NAFTA shows that this outcome is inconsistent with reality.

A natural way to avoid these extreme results is to cast the analysis in terms of a model with product differentiation. A fully satisfactory model of this type requires the introduction of economies of scale and monopolistic competition or oligopoly. Such an elaborate model is beyond the scope of this chapter. But taking recourse to the Armington structure whereby products are distinguished by the country of origin and drawing on the Meade (1955) model, we take a first stab at the problem.

An important point to note at the outset is that when products are differentiated by the country of origin, the small-country or small-union assumption must be abandoned.[22] If the product originating in a country is not produced anywhere else, by definition, the country is a monopolist for that product and cannot be a price taker in the world market.[23] Our approach below is to first consider the implications of FTAs at constant border prices and then bring in the effects of changes in the terms of trade.

---

22. This simple point seems to have escaped a number of CGE-modelers of NAFTA who distinguish products by the country of origin and continue to impose the small-country assumption.

23. The same would also hold true if we were to use a monopolistic-competition or oligopoly model.

FIGURE 1–5
EFFECT OF A SMALL TARIFF PREFERENCE BY COUNTRY A TO COUNTRY B

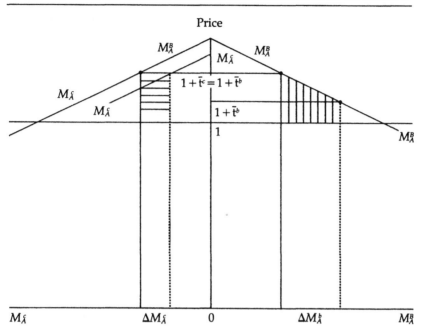

NOTE: Starting with equal tariffs, $\bar{t}^b = \bar{t}^c$, the tariff on product b is reduced by a small amount. Assuming all goods (including the exportable) to be substitutes, this change increases the imports of product b, reduces those of product c, and increases exports, all measured at world prices that are set equal to 1 by appropriate choice of units. The increase in imports of b, ΔM_A^b, leads to a welfare gain measured by the vertically shaded area while the decrease in imports of c, ΔM_A^c, leads to a welfare loss measured by the horizontally shaded area. For a small change in the tariff, both of these areas are approximated by rectangles formed by the change in imports and the height of the initial tariff. This means that the rectangle with the larger base is bigger. Because exports rise, the trade balance condition implies that there is a net expansion of imports. Thus, ΔM_A^b is larger than ΔM_A^c leading to the conclusion that the vertically shaded area is bigger than the horizontally shaded area.

Assume that there are three products denoted a, b, and c. Countries A, B, and C specialize in and export a, b, and c, respectively. Choose the units of each product so that its international price is unity in the initial equilibrium. Focus as before on country A's welfare. In the initial equilibrium, let A impose a uniform tariff t per unit on imports from B and C.

In figure 1–5 we measure A's consumption of b to the right and

23

that of c to the left of the origin, O. Because b and c are not produced in A, the demand curves also represent import demands. Given the tariff t on b and c, (import) demand curves are represented by $M_A{}^b M_A{}^b$ and $M_A{}^c M_A{}^c$. The demand curve for each product is drawn given the tariff rate on the other product. Assuming substitutability, a reduction in the tariff on one product shifts the demand curve for the other product toward the vertical axis.

Let us now introduce preferential trading through a small reduction in the tariff on imports from B. Imports from B expand and generate a gain equal to $t_b \Delta M_A{}^b$ and approximated by the vertically shaded area in figure 1–5. This is trade creation. But the reduction in the tariff on b also causes an inward shift in the demand curve for c as shown by the dotted curve. There is trade diversion and a corresponding loss equal to $t_c \Delta M_A{}^c$ and approximated by the horizontally shaded area.[24]

Is there a net gain or loss to country A? The answer depends on the relative sizes of the two shaded areas. For a small change in the tariff, these areas are approximated by rectangles whose height equals t. Therefore, the gain is larger than the loss if and only if the increase in the value of imports of b at world prices is larger than the reduction in the value of imports of c.[25] If we now assume that the partner country's good, b, and A's export good, a, are substitutes in A's demand, the preferential reduction in the tariff lowers the consumption of good a and allows an expansion of exports. Working through the trade balance condition, we can see that the expansion of exports must expand total imports valued at world prices. That is to say, imports of b expand more than imports of c contract. The area associated with trade creation in figure 1–5 exceeds the area associated with trade diversion; the *introduction* of preferential trading is beneficial.

This result is attributed to Lipsey (1958) and hinges critically on substitutability between demands for the partner country's goods and exportables and constancy of the terms of trade. For the moment, let us make these assumptions and ask what happens as we continue to lower the tariff on good b, holding the tariff on good c unchanged.

---

24. In a small, open economy with tariffs as the only distortion, the change in welfare (real income) from an infinitesimally small change in any set of tariffs equals the change in tariff revenue evaluated at initial tariff rates (Eaton and Panagariya 1979). For an infinitesimally small change in the tariff on B, the vertically shaded area in figure 1–5 is the increase and the horizontally shaded area the decrease in tariff revenue measured at the original tariff rates.

25. Observe that the world price of each product is unity. Therefore, the base of the rectangle represents both the quantity and value of imports at world prices.

FIGURE 1–6
EFFECT OF PREFERENTIAL TARIFF REDUCTION AND WELFARE

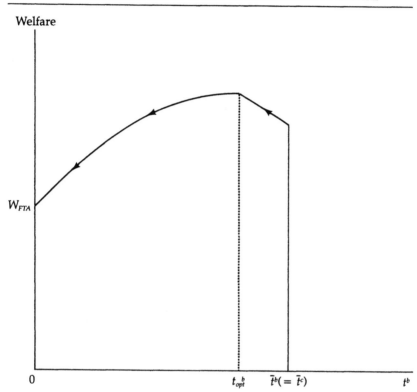

For each successive reduction in the tariff, the height of the rectangle associated with trade creation declines but that of the rectangle associated with trade diversion remains unchanged. Sooner or later, before the tariff on b goes to zero, the gain from extra trade creation becomes smaller than the loss from extra trade diversion. Further reductions in the tariff lead to a *reduction* in welfare.[26]

In sum, assuming constant terms of trade and substitutability between imports from B and exports, a preferential reduction in the tariff on B's goods first improves welfare and then lowers it. This relationship is shown in figure 1–6. As drawn, the level of welfare with a com-

---

26. To make this point another way, start with a zero tariff on good b and a positive tariff on c. The introduction of a small tariff on b will not lead to an efficiency loss in the b market but will generate an efficiency cost in the c market.

plete FTA is lower than that in the initial equilibrium. But in general, we cannot tell whether welfare rises or falls upon the establishment of an FTA.

The natural question then is whether we can establish a presumption one way or the other. To answer it, let us examine the second-best optimum tariff in the Meade model on B's goods given the tariff on C's goods. As shown in Panagariya (1996b), this tariff can be written as

$$\frac{t^b_{opt}}{1 + t^b_{opt}} = \frac{\bar{t^c}}{1 + \bar{t^c}} \cdot \frac{1}{1 + \dfrac{\eta_{ba}}{\eta_{bc}}},$$

where η_{ba} and η_{bc} are country A's compensated, crossprice elasticities of demand for the partner country's good with respect to the price of its own good and that of the outside country's good, respectively. These elasticities respectively measure the degree of substitutability between the partner's and A's own goods and that between the partner's and outside country's goods.

If the two elasticities are equal, the optimum tariff on b is approximately half of the tariff on c. In applying this model and argument to the real world, it is reasonable to expect, however, that the degree of substitutability is substantially higher between the imports from the two sources, B and C, than that between imports from B and A's exportables. For instance, Chile's imports from North America are likely to exhibit a much greater degree of substitutability with goods from the European Union or East Asia than with its own exports. Given this fact, the optimum tariff on b is higher than one-half of the tariff on the outside country's goods. In the limit, if the cross-price elasticity of demand for B with respect to the price of A is zero, the optimum tariff on b equals the initial tariff on c. In terms of figure 1–5, exports do not change at all when preferential trading is introduced and trade diversion exactly offsets trade creation. In terms of figure 1–6, welfare falls monotonically as we lower the tariff on b while holding the tariff on c constant.

The analysis up to this point has assumed that the terms of trade are constant, and it does not allow for the tariff-revenue-redistribution effect discussed earlier.[27] As already noted, with goods differentiated by the country of origin, the terms of trade cannot be assumed constant. The derivation of the effects of preferential trading on the terms

---

27. The effects shown in figure 1–5 do not arise in the partial equilibrium model of figures 1–2 and 1–3. Because these effects require the presence of at least two importables, they do not arise even in a two-good general equilibrium model.

of trade in the three-good model is complicated. Fortunately, in a neglected but important paper, these effects were worked out by Robert Mundell. To quote him,

> (1) A discriminatory tariff reduction by a member country improves the terms of trade of the partner country with respect to both the tariff reducing country and the rest of the world, but the terms of trade of the tariff-reducing country might rise or fall with respect to third countries.
> (2) The degree of improvement in the terms of trade of the partner country is likely to be larger the greater is the member's tariff reduction; this establishes the presumption that a member's gain from a free-trade area will be larger the higher are initial tariffs of partner countries (Mundell 1964, 8).

Not surprisingly, once the terms-of-trade changes are brought back into the analysis, the "mercantilist" bias in results noted earlier (that is, that A loses from its own liberalization) comes back even in the Meade model.[28] We are once again driven to the conclusion that a high-protection country (Mexico) forming an FTA with a low-protection country (United States) is likely to lose from the FTA. Observe that the terms-of-trade effects are in addition to the likely losses from second-best considerations at fixed terms of trade as discussed in figures 1–5 and 1–6.

Revenue Seeking. The conclusion that a country is likely to lose from its own preferential liberalization can break down in the presence of 100 percent, perfectly competitive, resource-using revenue-seeking activities.[29] Given this type of revenue seeking, each dollar's worth of tariff revenue will be matched by a dollar's worth of real resources used unproductively. The tariff revenue is represented by the rectangle GHNS in figure 1–2, where A and B form the FTA. This revenue is now lost in revenue seeking and will not contribute to the country's welfare. The introduction of preferential trading will then lead to a loss of tariff revenue in the amount GFLH, but it will generate an exactly equivalent gain from a release of resources employed in revenue seeking, leaving A's welfare unchanged. For the union as a whole, however, the re-

---

28. Recall that in figures 1–1 and 1–2, the *internal* terms of trade are variable. Country A's terms of trade with respect to country B deteriorate by the full amount of the tariff reduction. But because of the small-union assumption, the external terms of trade do not change there.

29. One hundred percent revenue seeking means that the entire revenue is available for those who wish to seek it. Perfectly competitive revenue seeking leads to a dollar's worth of resource loss for a dollar of revenue sought. The

duced revenue seeking will generate a net gain equal to GFLH. A large part of this gain, trapezium GFUH, will go to the partner country B, while the remaining part, triangle UFL, pays for the cost of trade diversion. In sum, country A's welfare does not change while that of B rises.

Next, consider the case in figure 1–3 where A and C have the FTA instead. Once again, the rectangle GSNH now will not contribute to the country's welfare in the initial equilibrium. But when preferential liberalization is introduced, the internal price of A falls to the level shown by point R and the rectangle (plus triangle SNR) becomes a part of the consumers' surplus and hence A's welfare rises. Country B's welfare does not change.

Combining the two cases, we obtain the conclusion that, in the presence of 100 percent perfectly competitive revenue seeking, each partner benefits unambiguously (or at least does not lose) from preferential trading. This conclusion undermines our argument that preferential liberalization by a country with respect to its major trading partner is likely to hurt itself and benefit its partner.

We suggest, however, that there are at least two reasons why we should not take this conclusion seriously. First, even though revenue seeking is an important phenomenon in certain contexts and worthy of analysis in its own right, it is hardly invoked when making major policy decisions. We are not aware of a single reference to revenue seeking as a major reason for NAFTA in the public debate in either Mexico or the United States and Canada preceding its approval. Indeed, if we are to take revenue seeking seriously, we should take it and other types of directly unproductive profit-seeking (DUP) activities arising from all other policies into account as well. Second, the twin assumptions of 100 percent and perfectly competitive revenue seeking are unrealistic. Empirically, revenue seeking is likely for several reasons to be a small fraction of the total revenue. In particular, the operation of the "Brother-in-Law Theorem" and of settled rules for allocation of revenues will often turn potential DUP activities into transfers.

"Natural Trading Partners" Hypothesis and Regional PTAs. We now turn to the question of natural trading partners.[30] As we noted earlier, the "natural trading partners" phrasing and hypothesis (that PTAs among them are more likely to beneficial) originated in Wonnacott and

---

two assumptions together imply that the resources used up in revenue seeking equal the tariff revenues in equilibrium. For rent seeking, see Krueger (1974) and for revenue seeking, see Bhagwati and Srinivasan (1980).

30. A detailed, general equilibrium analysis of this issue is provided in Panagariya (1996a, 1996b).

Lutz (1989). Based on the work of Viner (1950), Lipsey (1960), and John-son (1962), these authors provided detailed criteria for determining whether or not a given set of countries constituted natural trading part-ners:

> Trade creation is likely to be great, and trade diversion small, if the prospective members of an FTA are natural trading partners. Several points are relevant:
> • Are the prospective members already major trading part-ners? If so, the FTA will be reinforcing natural trading part-ners, not artificially diverting them.
> • Are the prospective members close geographically? Groupings of distant nations may be economically inefficient because of the high transportation costs (Wonnacott and Lutz 1989, 69).

Wonnacott and Lutz offered two further criteria, one based on comple-mentarity versus competitiveness of the economies and the other on the countries' relative levels of economic development. They noted, however, that these characteristics are "much more difficult to evalu-ate." Because subsequent advocates of FTAs have not included these criteria in defining natural trading partners, we will not discuss them.

For clarity, we will refer to the first two criteria spelled out in the above passage from Wonnacott and Lutz as the "volume-of-trade" and "transport-cost" criteria and examine them in turn.

The volume-of-trade criterion. The volume-of-trade criterion for choosing natural trading partners and treating them as likely therefore to be welfare enhancing to their members seems plausible at first glance but is, in fact, treacherous for several reasons.

First, the criterion is neither symmetric nor transitive. A lack of symmetry implies that country A may be a natural trading partner of country B, but the reverse may not hold true. A lack of transitivity implies that even if A is a natural trading partner of B, and B is a natural trading partner of C, A may not be a natural trading partner of C. Lest this be viewed as a purely academic point, we note that the United States is Mexico's largest trading partner, but the reverse is not true. Similarly, the United States is the largest trading partner of both Canada and Mexico, but Canada and Mexico have little trade with each other.

Second, the volume-of-trade criterion is premised on the view that a larger initial volume of trade between potential partners implies a lower likelihood of loss because of trade diversion. In terms of figure 1–2, this implies that the larger is OQ_1, the smaller is Q_1Q_2.

This is, however, an unsupported inference from the fact that, for any given volume of initial imports (OQ_3), the higher is the partner country's initial share, the lower is the outside country's share and hence the smaller is the *scope* for diverting trade. Instead, what one needs to determine is how likely is the *actual* trade diversion. (Thus, for example, between two alternate situations, one where Q_1Q_3 [the scope for trade diversion] is twice as large as in the other, Q_1Q_2 (the actual trade diversion) could still be only half as much.)

The underlying model that defines the trade volumes in different equilibriums may well imply then that the relationship between the initial volume of imports from the partner country and the trade to be diverted to it may be altogether tenuous.

Thus, consider the Lipsey (1958) analysis of the question, based on the small-union version of the Meade model we have discussed.[31] Lipsey, as Bhagwati recalled in his earlier critique of the volume-of-trade criterion, focused not on the initial volume of imports but "on the relative sizes of imports from each source vis-à-vis expenditure on domestic goods as the key and decisive factor in determining the size of losses and gains from the preferential cuts in trade barriers" (Bhagwati 1993a, 34). Of course, on the basis of equation 1 and the discussion of it, we can also conclude that, in general in this model, the higher is the compensated crossprice elasticity of its demand for the partner's good with respect to the price of its own good *relative* to the crossprice elasticity of its demand for the good with respect to the price of the outside country's good, the higher is the likelihood that an FTA improves a country's welfare. This general conclusion reduces to the Lipsey argument when the liberalizing country's preferences are of the CES variety.[32]

---

31. We assumed earlier that each country is the sole producer of its export good. This assumption necessarily makes the terms of trade variable. In the conventional analysis, as also in the present discussion, the outside country is assumed to produce all goods and is large. The terms of trade are then determined in the outside country, and the only effects that arise are those depicted in figure 1–5. In arriving at the conclusions discussed in this paragraph, Lipsey also assumed that preferences are Cobb-Douglas. For further details, see Panagariya (1996a, 1996b).

32. As quoted in footnote 12 of Bhagwati (1993a), according to Lipsey, "the larger are purchases of domestic commodities and the smaller are purchases from the outside world, the more likely is it that the union will bring gain." If the liberalizing country's preferences are of the CES variety, the compensated crossprice elasticity of its demand for the partner's good with respect to the price of its own good reduces to the product of the expenditure share of its own good and the elasticity of substitution. A similar statement applies to the compensated crossprice elasticity of the country's demand for the partner's good with respect to the price of the outside country's good. Thus, under CES preferences, our condition in the text reduces to Lipsey's. As noted in the previous footnote, Lipsey himself had relied on Cobb-Douglas preferences to derive the conclusion quoted at the beginning of this footnote.

For a country such as Mexico joining the NAFTA with the United States, we may well expect in fact the former elasticity to be lower than the latter so that the welfare presumption for this "natural trading partner" of the United States from NAFTA is ironically likely to be in favor of trade-diversion effects dominating the outcome.

There is a further subtle point to be noted. In figure 1–6, starting from a nondiscriminatory tariff, as country A lowers the tariff on B, trade share shifts in favor of B at the expense of country C. That is, A and B become more natural trading partners according to the volume-of-trade criterion. Yet, once the tariff on B attains the second-best optimum, t^b_{opt}, further preferential liberalization is accompanied by a *reduction* in the welfare of A. Thus, to the left of t^b_{opt}, A and B are more natural trading partners than to the right of it, but preferential tariff reductions in that range reduce welfare.

Third, even this conclusion understates the folly of regarding a large initial volume of imports as a benign phenomenon. It ignores the crucial tariff-revenue-redistribution effect that we have highlighted. In FTAs involving countries with asymmetric levels of protection and a high volume of trade initially, the country with higher protection is likely to lose even if trade-creation effects dominate trade-diversion effects. Under such circumstances, the net gain from trade-creation and trade-diversion effects could likely be swamped by the loss from the tariff-revenue-redistribution effect. The case for Mexico gaining from joining NAFTA thus looks dismal on this account as well.

While, therefore, the volume-of-trade criterion for judging FTAs to be benign is clearly to be rejected, linking it to *regionalism* and thus declaring regional FTAs to be more benign than nonregional FTAs is additionally wrong. There is no evidence at all that pairs of contiguous countries, or countries with common borders, have larger volumes of trade with each other than do pairs that are not so situated or that trade volumes of pairs of countries, arranged by distance between the countries in the pair, will show distance to be inversely related to trade volumes.[33]

This is evident from the somewhat aggregated destination-related trade volume statistics for major regions in 1980, 1985, and 1990 in table 1–3.[34] Then again, take just one telling example.[35] Chile shares a

33. This would not be generally true even if we were to take the measure just for one individual country with every other country instead of pooling all possible pairs together.

34. Thus, intra-African exports were only 12.8 percent of total African exports in 1990.

35. There are countless other examples. Bhagwati (1993a) cites India-Pakistan versus India-United Kingdom and India-USSR as an example.

TABLE 1-3
DIRECTION OF EXPORTS BY MAJOR REGIONS, 1980, 1985, AND 1990

Exporter	Year	North America	Western Europe	Europe	East Asia[a]	Latin America	Africa	Middle East	South Asia
North America	1980	33.5	25.2	27.4	15.8	8.9	3.3	4.2	1.0
	1985	44.4	19.3	21.0	15.5	5.9	2.5	3.2	1.0
	1990	41.9	22.3	23.4	20.4	5.0	1.7	2.6	0.8
Western Europe	1980	6.7	67.1	71.9	2.9	2.4	7.2	5.5	0.7
	1985	11.3	64.9	68.9	3.6	1.6	5.2	5.0	0.9
	1990	8.3	71.0	74.4	5.3	1.1	3.3	3.3	0.7
Europe	1980	6.3	63.7	72.7	2.7	2.3	6.9	5.5	0.7
	1985	11.0	63.5	69.2	3.4	1.6	5.1	5.0	0.9
	1990	8.2	70.6	74.5	5.2	1.1	3.3	3.3	0.7
East Asia	1980	26.0	16.8	18.9	29.9	4.1	4.4	7.4	1.8
	1985	37.8	13.6	15.5	25.3	2.8	2.2	5.1	2.0
	1990	31.9	19.8	20.7	32.3	1.9	1.6	3.0	1.5

Region	Year								
Latin America	1980	27.9	26.5	35.1	5.4	16.6	2.7	1.9	0.5
	1985	35.8	25.9	30.4	7.1	12.1	3.7	3.0	0.7
	1990	22.9	25.3	27.6	10.3	14.0	2.1	2.4	0.4
Africa	1980	27.4	43.6	46.1	4.3	3.2	1.8	1.7	0.3
	1985	14.8	64.9	69.3	1.8	4.2	5.1	2.2	0.7
	1990	3.0	66.0	68.0	4.6	0.6	12.8	4.4	3.6
Middle East	1980	11.5	40.3	41.5	28.7	5.0	1.5	4.1	2.5
	1985	6.2	15.0	17.7	1.5	0.3	1.4	8.7	0.4
	1990	17.8	48.6	53.0	9.1	1.2	3.6	8.5	0.9
South Asia	1980	10.9	24.6	39.4	14.5	0.5	6.8	14.5	5.6
	1985	18.4	20.8	37.0	16.4	0.4	4.6	11.0	4.4
	1990	17.1	30.1	46.6	18.3	0.3	2.7	6.5	3.2

a. East Asia does not include China.
NOTE: This table broadly underlines the point that *total* trade volumes that matter do not show any relationship to proximity of countries geographically.
SOURCE: Panagariya (1993). He cites U.N. COMTRADE data.

common border with Argentina, but in 1993 it shipped only 6.2 percent of exports to Argentina and received only 5 percent of its imports from her (Panagariya 1995b, tables 3 and 4). By contrast, the United States does not have a common border with Chile but in 1993 accounted for 16.2 percent of her exports and 24.9 percent of her imports. The volume-of-trade criterion then would make the United States, *not* Argentina, the natural trading partner of Chile, clearly controverting the claim that the volume-of-trade criterion translates into a regional criterion.

As contended by Bhagwati (1993a), the equation by Krugman (1991) and Summers (1991a) of the two concepts of volume of trade and regionalism (whether of the distance or the common border or contiguity variety) is therefore simply wrong.

Nonetheless, Frankel and Wei (1995) have recently argued otherwise, claiming that their empirical work favors the Krugman-Summers assertion. They use the gravity model as their basic tool to conclude that "proximity is in general an important determinant of bilateral trade around the world, notwithstanding exceptions like India-Pakistan and other cases."

But this misses the point at issue. What is at stake is not whether distance, interpreted through the gravity model and/or common border modeled through a dummy, matters.[36] There does seem to be a *partial* correlation between distance, proximity, common border, and so on, on the one hand, and trade volumes on the other.[37] But what we have to look at is the *total* initial volume of trade, and this does not correlate simply with distance as the right-hand side variable, as required by the "natural trading partners" assertion of the volume-of-trade criterion for forming PTAs.

Next, we have the difficult problem of endogeneity of initial trade

---

36. Although Frankel and Wei find that a common border increases trade volumes, Dhar and Panagariya (1994), who estimate the gravity equation on a country-by-country basis for twenty-two countries, find the common-border effect to be negative in six cases. This conflict of results underlies the serious reservations we have about the use of these gravity models to infer "trade diversion," and so on: the coefficients vary considerably depending on the dataset, and sometimes the signs do as well.

37. We note, however, that the recent critique of gravity models by Jacques J. Polak (1996) casts serious doubt on even this conclusion. Polak estimates a gravity equation for total imports as a function of income, population, and a location index measuring how favorably a country is located for purposes of international trade. He finds that, for 1960 trade data, the location index yields a statistically significant effect, as in Frankel-Wei regressions. But for the 1990 sample used by Frankel and Wei, the effect is statistically insignificant.

volumes with respect to preferences. If the large volumes are themselves attributable, in significant degree, to preferences granted earlier, then they are not "natural," nor is it proper to think that additional preferences are "therefore" harmless. The point is best understood by thinking of high trade barriers by a country leading to a larger within-country trade relative to external trade. To deduce that added barriers are harmless is to compound the harm done by existing barriers that are, of course, preferences in favor of trade within the country.

This is not an idle question. Offshore assembly provisions between the United States and Mexico and the longstanding GATT-sanctioned free trade regime in autos between Canada and the United States are certainly not negligible factors in pre-NAFTA U.S. trade with these NAFTA members. In granting preferences under the Generalized System of Preferences, the United States, EC, and Japan have all concentrated on their regions. Thus, the partial correlation between distance and trade volumes (in gravity models) may be a result of preferences granted to proximate neighbors, rather than a "natural" phenomenon justifying (new) preferences.[38]

Finally, we need to raise a different objection to the argument that a high initial volume of imports from a partner country will work to protect a country against trade diversion. Quite aside from the fact that aggregate volumes shift significantly in practice over time, the comparative advantage in specific goods and services often changes in different locations.[39] Consistent with a given aggregate trade volume, its composition may shift so as to yield greater trade diversion when a PTA is present.

Consider a case, based on constant costs for simplicity, in which the United States imports a product from Canada under a nondiscriminatory tariff. If a PTA is formed between the two countries, the product will continue to be imported from Canada. But suppose that, on a future date, Canada loses its comparative advantage to Taiwan ever so slightly so that the preferential advantage enjoyed by her outweighs this loss. There will be trade diversion, and imports into the United States will continue to come from Canada with the volume of trade

---

38. Of course, even if the relationship was "natural," it does not justify preferences as argued already by us.

39. Bhagwati, in several writings, for example, Bhagwati and Dehejia (1994) and Bhagwati (1996a), has argued that comparative advantage has become "kaleidoscopic," that is, thin and volatile, as technical know-how has converged, multinationals have become global, interest rates have become closer across nations, and access to different capital markets has become more open. More and more industries are thus footloose.

remaining unchanged.[40] Observe that there is an asymmetry here between a shift in comparative advantage away from the partner and that toward it. If Canada experiences a reduction in the cost of production of a product imported by the United States from Taiwan under a PTA, there can still be trade diversion. Because of the preference, Canada will replace Taiwan as the supplier of this product even before Canada's costs fall below those of Taiwan. The volume of trade will rise, and at the same time there will be trade diversion.[41] The proponents of the complacent "high volume of imports" thesis are thus trapped in a static view of comparative advantage that is particularly at odds with today's volatile, "kaleidoscopic" comparative advantage in the global economy.

Transport-cost criterion. But if the volume-of-trade criterion is conceptually inappropriate and must be summarily rejected, what about the transport-cost criterion? This criterion maps directly into distance and hence into regionalism. However, the question to be analyzed is: should PTA partners be chosen on the basis of lower transport costs, and hence greater proximity, to maximize gains to members or to minimize losses to them?

The earliest reference we could find to transport costs in the context of trade liberalization is from Johnson (1962, 61): "If the separate markets of various members are divided by serious geographical barriers which require high transport costs to overcome them, the enlargement of the market may be more apparent than real." All he seemed to be arguing was the truism that trade liberalization may be meaningless if high transport costs prevented trade from breaking out.

But the natural trading partners hypothesis is altogether different and incorrect. There is, in fact, no reason to think that greater distance increases the likelihood of gain for members in a PTA. This can be seen simply by constructing a counterexample where a union with a country (C) that is more distant produces more gain (for A) than a union with the country (B) that is less distant but otherwise identical (to C).

First note that as long as country A in figure 1–2 imports the good from both B and C in the pre- and post-FTA equilibrium, the presence of transportation costs has no effect whatsoever on the analysis based on that figure. All we need to do is to imagine that the supply price of C is inclusive of transport costs, while such costs are absent for the

---

40. In this paragraph, we abstract from the demand effects. The inclusion of demand effects will modify the discussion but not the fundamental point.

41. And if costs indeed fall below those of Taiwan, there is no extra gain from the PTA since in that case Canada would have replaced Taiwan as the supplier even under a nondiscriminatory tariff.

FIGURE 1-7
EXAMPLE OF POSITIVE EFFECTS OF UNION WITH A MORE DISTANT
COUNTRY

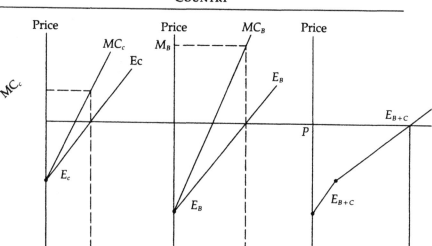

partner, B. This introduction of transport costs leaves the remainder of the analysis entirely unchanged.

To construct the counterexample noted above, consider a world consisting of three countries: A, B, and C. Country A has the option to form an FTA with either B or C. Countries B and C are identical in all respects except that the latter is located farther. If the supply curves of B and C were horizontal, we would be in a world represented in panel a of figure 1–1 with $(P_C - P_B)$ representing transportation costs from C to A. Technically, in this case an FTA with the geographically proximate B improves A's welfare. But recall the limitation of such an FTA: country A does not trade with C before or after the union is formed; and in the post-FTA equilibrium, the external tariff does not matter so the FTA is really equivalent to nondiscriminatory free trade.

To make the example substantive, we must therefore assume that supply curves of B and C are upward sloped.[42] In figure 1–7, we draw three panels. In the first two panels, we show the export supply curves of C and B as $E_C E_C$ and $E_B E_B$, respectively. In the third panel, we have their combined supply obtained by summing horizontally the individ-

---

42. This makes the analysis complicated because the countries now wield market power, and unilateral free trade is no longer optimal.

ual supplies from the first two panels. The supply curves of C and B are identical in all respects except that C's supply price includes a constant per-unit transportation cost. Thus, for each quantity, C's supply price exceeds that of B by the per-unit transportation cost.[43]

To avoid clutter, we do not draw A's demand curve. Instead, imagine that there is an arbitrary nondiscriminatory tariff initially that yields the total demand for imports as represented by point Q_{B+C}. The price paid for this quantity to B and C is P^*. Individual supplies of B and C can be obtained by intersecting their supply curves with P^* and are shown by Q_B and Q_C. Not surprisingly, imports are larger from the geographically proximate country B than from C.

Now consider the introduction of preferential trading. To see which way preferences should be given, draw the *marginal* cost curve associated with each supply curve. These are shown by MC_B and MC_C. It is then immediate that, at the initial nondiscriminatory tariff, the marginal cost of imports is higher on imports from B than from C. We then obtain the dramatic conclusion that if A wants to give a tariff preference, it should opt for the distant partner C rather than the proximate B! The transport-cost criterion for choosing partners in a PTA is exactly wrong in this instance.

The explanation of this result is straightforward. The discriminating monopsonist model says that for any quantity of total purchases, the supplier with higher elasticity should be paid a higher price. In the present problem, this prescription translates into a lower tax on the supplier with higher elasticity. And transportation costs make C's supply curve more elastic than that of B.

Endogenous Tariffs on the Outside Country. So far, we have assumed that when an FTA is formed, the tariff on the outside country is held at its original level. But this may not always be true. When an FTA begins to take a bite, lobbies representing declining domestic industries may be able to reassert themselves. Because the FTA ties the authorities' hands with respect to the union partner, they will have to respond by raising protection against outside countries. This, indeed, happened recently following the Mexican crisis when the country raised external tariffs on 502 products from 20 percent or less to 35 percent!

This possibility had been anticipated by Bhagwati (1993a, 36–37). He wrote:

---

43. The point can also be made under "iceberg" type transport costs that are frequently employed in international trade literature. In this formulation, a constant fraction of the good melts away in transit.

Imagine that the United States begins to eliminate (by out competing) an inefficient Mexican industry once the FTA goes into effect. Even though the most efficient producer is Taiwan, if the next efficient United States out competes the least efficient Mexico, that would be desirable trade creation. . . .

But what would the Mexicans be likely to do? They would probably start AD actions against Taiwan.

This possibility raises the questions whether, once we allow for endogenous policy response, welfare may actually decline relative to the FTA and, indeed, to the initial equilibrium. Answers to both questions are in the affirmative.

A simple example demonstrating welfare deterioration relative to the FTA can be given as follows. For a zero tariff on B, calculate A's optimum tariff on C. Suppose that A sets the initial, nondiscriminatory tariff on B and C at this level. Then, by construction, an FTA with B, holding C's tariff unchanged, not only improves A's welfare but actually maximizes it. If now lobbying pressure leads to a rise in the external tariff, A's welfare will necessarily fall.

The more interesting is the possibility that A's welfare can decline relative to the initial, pre-FTA equilibrium. To demonstrate it, note that A's welfare can be written as

$$W = CS + PS + t_B P_B{}^* M_B + t_C P_C{}^* M_C$$
$$= CS + PS + (P - P_B{}^*)M_B + (P - P_C{}^*)M_C$$
$$= CS + PS + P(M_B + M_C) - (P_B{}^* M_B + P_C{}^* M_C),$$

where CS denotes A's consumers' surplus, PS its producers' surplus, P domestic price, $P_i{}^*$ ($i = $ B, C) border price on imports from i, t_i the *ad valorem* tariff on imports from i, and M_i imports from i. The last two terms in these equalities represent tariff revenue on imports. Given a nondiscriminatory tariff initially, $P_B{}^* = P_C{}^*$.

Take the case favorable to an FTA with B by assuming that at each world price, B's supply is more elastic than C's. Assume further that the initial, nondiscriminatory tariff is sufficiently high that the FTA with no change in the tariff on C is welfare improving for A.[44] We will now show that if, because of lobbying pressure, the FTA is accompanied by a rise in the tariff on C such that *total* imports are unchanged, it is possible for its welfare to decline. Given that the FTA with no change in the tariff on C is welfare improving, this result shows that the endogenous tariff response can turn a welfare-improving FTA into a welfare-reducing proposition.

---

44. If the initial tariff is above the optimum tariff, given the elasticity assumption, a small preferential reduction in the tariff on B is welfare improving. For a complete removal of the tariff on B to be welfare improving, the initial tariff must be substantially higher than the optimum tariff.

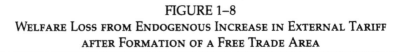

FIGURE 1–8
WELFARE LOSS FROM ENDOGENOUS INCREASE IN EXTERNAL TARIFF
AFTER FORMATION OF A FREE TRADE AREA

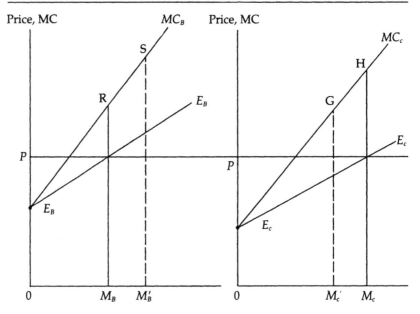

With no change in imports, the domestic price in A does not change and neither do *CS* and *PS*. From equation 2, it is then clear that welfare will rise or fall as the cost of imports, represented by the last term in the last equality, falls or rises. This property allows us to analyze the impact of the endogenous choice of the tariff by focusing on import supplies from B and C only.

In figure 1–8, as assumed, B's export-supply curve is more elastic than that of C at each price. This means that under a nondiscriminatory tariff, A's *private* marginal cost of obtaining imports from B is lower than that from C. Therefore, *at the margin*, A benefits by switching imports from C to B.

Initially, with a nondiscriminatory tariff, A buys the product at P^* per-unit from both B and C. Imports from the two countries are given by M_B and M_C, respectively. The marginal cost of obtaining imports from B is less than that from C, $RM_B < HM_C$. As noted in the previous paragraph, at the margin, switching imports from C to B is beneficial to A: a small reduction in the tariff on B and increase in tariff on C which keeps total imports unchanged is welfare improving. But the FTA requires taking the tariff on B all the way to 0. As that is done, the marginal cost of obtaining imports from B rises, and as we correspondingly raise the tariff on C to keep the total imports unchanged, the marginal cost of imports from C falls. It is entirely possible that the two marginal costs cross and then reach levels such that the total cost of imports actually rises. Figure 1–8 is drawn on the assumption that the FTA increases imports from B by $M_B M_B'$. The tariff on C has to be raised to reduce imports from that country by an equivalent amount shown by $M_C M_C'$. As drawn, the net change in the cost of imports, $SRM_B M_B' - GHM_C M_C'$, is positive indicating that welfare declines.[45]

Welfare Loss without Trade Diversion. The general impression in the literature is that a welfare loss from an FTA can arise only if there is trade diversion. It is easy to show, however, that a welfare loss to an *individual* member (though not to the union as a whole nor to the world) can arise even if there is no trade diversion. The simplest example of this phenomenon can be gleaned from figure 1–2. Starting from a nondiscriminatory tariff, marginal costs of production in B and C are equal. Given that *at the margin* both B and C are equally efficient suppliers of the product, there can be no trade diversion if we lower the tariff on B by an infinitesimally small amount. Yet because A's terms of trade with respect to B deteriorate by the full amount of the tariff reduction, it will lose from such a change.

In figure 1–2, because the domestic price does not change after the introduction of preferential trading, there is no trade creation. But if we allow C's supply curve to slope upward, the introduction of a small tariff preference for B will also generate a trade-creation effect. This is because the preference improves A's terms of trade with respect to C, lowers the domestic price, and displaces some inefficient domestic production. For reasons explained in the previous paragraph, there is no trade diversion, however. Yet it is possible for the loss from the accompanying deterioration in the terms of trade vis-à-vis B to more than offset the gain from trade creation as well as the improvement in the terms of trade vis-à-vis C (a result that can be derived algebraically, of course).

Concluding against PTAs. Our analysis of the static effects of PTAs is far less sanguine than is customarily assumed by several policy economists, bureaucrats, and politicians today. It also challenges and undermines the validity of the claims made in behalf of "regional" PTAs, whether the regions are defined in terms of countries with relatively high intraregional trade or in terms of proximity with or without common borders.

---

45. De Melo, Panagariya, and Rodrik (1993) note a similar possibility when the country faces a revenue constraint.

Therefore, if we were to assume that PTAs result from a variety of noneconomic factors, we need not be complacent about the possibility of their resulting in harmful effects.[46] Nor would there be any good reason to be complacent even if those PTAs were to be essentially regional in scope, when "regional" means geographic proximity or higher volumes of trade among, rather than outside, members.

We add three final observations. First, the common usage by journalists and politicians of the word "regional" frequently includes "common-ocean" arrangements such as APEC. Remember that APEC includes both South Korea and Chile, countries whose mutual trade is characterized by smallness of volume *and* largeness of distance, so that neither of the two criteria of distance or volume of trade for sanctifying PTAs as desirable, inappropriate as we have shown it to be, holds for every member of APEC vis-à-vis every other.

Second, is the presence of common waters a new criterion for getting nations to form a PTA (the Pacific Ocean in the case of APEC)? We should not forget that the major oceans, and hence most of the trading nations of the world, are united by the world's water, and even more readily thanks to the Suez and Panama canals! In fact, the fullest-bodied common-waters "regional" area is clearly approximated by the membership of the WTO, as would have been appreciated by Ferdinand Magellan, who starting out from San Lucar in 1519 sailed from the Atlantic into the Pacific, an ocean unknown at the time.[47]

Third, the term "continental trading arrangements" has also been frequently used by Wei and Frankel (1995), who argue that "many [trading blocs] are along continental lines".[48] But this is at best misleading and at worst incorrect. Even if we confine ourselves to Article XXIV-sanctioned arrangements, we still must distinguish among PTAs that are continentwide and hence "continental," those that cut across continents and are thus "intercontinental," and those that consist of members entirely *within*, but are not extended to *all* countries in, a continent and hence must be called "subcontinental."

---

46. We discuss these noneconomic factors later in the chapter. Our analysis, which has focused mainly on the effects on the member countries, has not addressed adequately the issue of the effects on nonmembers. However, there is a revival of interest in that issue as well. See, in particular, Srinivasan (1995) and Winters (1995a, 1995b).

47. The common-water definition, of course, excludes land-locked countries such as Nepal and countries with shores only on land-locked seas such as the Caspian. These, however, add up to only a small fraction of world trade. See Bhagwati (1996b) for more on common-waters FTAs.

48. Also see Frankel, Stein, and Wei (1995a, 1995b). Interestingly, Haberler (1943) appears to have been the first to use the term *continental blocs*.

Geographers and earth scientists divide the earth traditionally into four oceans (Arctic, Indian, Atlantic, and Pacific) and seven continents (Europe, Asia, Africa, Australia, North America, South America, and Antarctica). Only NAFTA and the PTA between Australia and New Zealand can then qualify as continental. And, the major new Article XXIV-sanctioned PTAs, which have been proposed by different groups in recent years (NAFTA extension into South America, APEC, and TAFTA) and which would clearly dwarf the continental PTAs clearly cut across continents.[49] Then again, MERCOSUR and ASEAN are clearly subcontinental. Of course, if one adds all the non-Article XXIV preferential trading arrangements, the matter looks even worse for those who claim that "many" of today's "trade blocs" are "continental."

Theoretical Analysis of the Dynamic Time-Path Question

Our analysis of the economics of PTAs would be seriously incomplete if, having analyzed the static effects, we did not go on to analyze the dynamic time-path question.

Formulating the Time-Path Question. Essentially, this question relates not to whether the immediate (static) effect of a PTA is good or bad, but whether the (dynamic) effect of the PTA is to accelerate or decelerate the continued reduction of trade barriers toward the goal of reducing them worldwide. This question may be formulated analytically in two separate ways.

Question I. Assume that the time-path of MTN (multilateral trade negotiations) and the time-path of PTAs are separable and do not influence each other. The two policies are "strangers" to (that is, independent of) one another: neither hurts or helps the other. Will then the PTA time-path be characterized by stagnant or negligible expansion of membership? Or will we have expanding membership, with this even turning eventually into worldwide membership as in the WTO, thus arriving at nondiscriminatory free trade for all? A similar question can be raised for the MTN time-path. And the analysis can be extended to a comparison of the two time-paths, ranking the efficacy of the two methods of reducing trade barriers to achieve the goal of worldwide free trade for all.

---

49. As matters stand currently, however, APEC and TAFTA are extremely unlikely to become Article XXIV-sanctioned PTAs, despite the U.S. obsession with PTAs, whereas the extension of NAFTA to the South looks like a long-term process.

Question II. Assume instead, as is more sensible, that if both the MTN and the PTA time-paths are embraced simultaneously, they will interact. In particular, the policy of undertaking PTAs will have a malign impact on (be a "foe" of) the progress along the MTN time-path, or it will have a benign effect on (be a "friend" of) the MTN time-path.[50]

Question I can be illustrated with the aid of figure 1–9, which portrays a sample of possibilities for the time-paths in question. World (rather than individual member) welfare is put on the vertical axis and time along the horizontal axis. For the PTA time-paths drawn, an upward movement along the path implies growing membership; for the MTN (or what are described as "process-multilateralism") time-paths, it implies nondiscriminatory lowering of trade barriers among the nearly worldwide WTO membership instead. The PTA and MTN time-paths are assumed to be independent of each other; the PTA time-path neither accelerates nor decelerates the course of MTN (thus ruling out Question II-type issues). The goal can be treated as reaching U^*, the worldwide freeing of trade barriers on a nondiscriminatory basis at a specified time.

Question I can be illustrated by reference to the PTA paths I–IV. Thus, PTAs may improve welfare immediately, in the static sense, from U^0 to U_p^2 or reduce it to U_p^1. In either case, the time-path could then be stagnant (as with time-paths II and III), implying a fragmentation of the world economy through no further expansion of the initial PTA. Else, it can lead (as in time-paths I and IV) to multilateral free trade for all at U^* through continued expansion and coagulation of the PTAs. Under "process multilateralism," that is, MTN as a multilateral process of reducing trade barriers as distinct from multilateralism as the goal desired, the time-path may fail to reach U^* and instead fall short at U_m because of free-rider problems.

As indicated, if the PTA and MTN time-paths are interdependent, we can address Question II. In that case, the MTN time-path becomes a function of whether the PTA time-path is traveled simultaneously.

Question Originating in Policy. The dynamic time-path question has arisen, just as the static one did, in policy concerns and political decisions that ran ahead of the theory. The post-Vinerian, in-depth analysis of the static question coincided with the movement that eventually created the European Community through the Treaty of Rome in 1957. The dynamic time-path question has arisen in the context of the U.S.

---

50. Similarly, the MTN path may facilitate or obstruct the expansion of PTA membership, so that the interaction between the two paths may be mutual.

FIGURE 1–9

ALTERNATIVE TIME-PATHS UNDER MULTILATERALISM AND UNDER PTAS

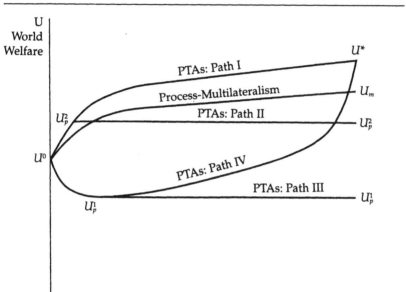

NOTE: This figure illustrates the "building blocks" and "stumbling blocks" concepts in the context of the question whether the regionalism (that is, PTAs) dynamic time-path will show increasing or stagnant membership.

The PTAs may improve welfare immediately from U^0 to U_p^2 or (because of net trade diversion) reduce it to U_p^1. The time-path with PTAs, in either case, could be stagnant (Paths II and III), implying a fragmentation of the world economy through no further expansion of the initial trade bloc. Or it could lead (Paths I and IV) to multilateral free trade for all at U^* through continued expansion and coagulation of PTAs. Under process-multilateralism, the time-path may fail to reach U^* and instead fall short at U_m because of free-rider problems. Or it may overcome them and reach U^*. This diagram assumes that the time-paths are independent: embarking on the PTAs path does not affect the process-multilateralism path. The text discusses such interdependence at length.

SOURCE: Adapted from Bhagwati (1993).

failure to get an MTN Round started at the GATT Ministerial in 1982 and the U.S. decision to finally abandon its studied avoidance of Article XXIV-sanctioned PTAs. The policy choice made was initially Hobson's choice: if the MTN could not be used to continue lowering trade barriers, then PTAs would be used instead. If the turnpike could not be used, one had no option except to use the dirt road.

For several reasons that have been systematically explored in Bhagwati (1993b), the United States ended, however, becoming committed to "walking on both legs," embracing both the PTA and the MTN paths. Indeed, the United States has now become an active proponent of this view, continuing to do so even after the Uruguay Round of MTN had been successfully conducted and the WTO launched. And, in doing so, its spokespersons have frequently implied that PTAs will have a benign, beneficial impact on the worldwide lowering of trade barriers through induced acceleration of MTN.

The questions that we have posed above spring from this shift in U.S. policy, which has been manifest for several years, starting from the Bush administration and articulated as a distinct policy in the Clinton administration. In Bhagwati (1991, 1993), the challenge to international trade theorists to analyze these questions was identified and a preliminary set of arguments offered. We recapitulate briefly those arguments and then review the theoretical literature that has been developing since then on the dynamic time-path questions.

"Exogenously Determined" Time-Paths: A Diversion. First, however, it is necessary to consider and to turn aside certain theoretical approaches that are not meaningful for thinking about the dynamic time-path questions at hand, even though they have often been mistaken to be so.

Kemp-Wan. The seminal approach of Kemp and Wan (1976) to Customs Union theory seems to be the most pertinent to our questions but, in fact, is not. Unlike the Vinerian approach, Kemp and Wan made the external tariff structure (of the Customs Union) endogenously chosen so that each member country's welfare would be improved, while that of the nonmembers was left unchanged. The beauty of this approach was that it restored, as it were, the commonsense intuition prior to Viner that a CU should be welfare improving for members and for the world. This is, of course, a "possibility" theorem, no more and no less.[51]

It is then immediately apparent that the PTA time-path to U^* in figure 1–9 can be made monotonic, provided expanding membership of a PTA always satisfies the Kemp-Wan rule for forming a Customs Union. But what this argument does not say, and indeed cannot say,

---

51. Christopher Bliss (1994) has tried to give the argument some structure. More recently, T. N. Srinivasan (1995) has done so in the context of examining the question of the impact of PTAs on nonmember welfare.

is that the PTA will necessarily expand and, if so, in this Kemp-Wan fashion.

For that answer, to what is obviously Question I, we must turn to the *incentive structure* that any CU/PTA provides, through interests, ideology, and institutions, for expansion or stagnation of its membership.

Krugman. The same argument applies to the theoretical approach to the question of PTAs recently introduced by Paul Krugman (1991a, 1991b, 1993). Again the expansion of membership is treated as exogenously specified, as in Viner, and the welfare consequences of the world mechanically dividing into a steadily increasing number of symmetric blocs—clearly demarcated countries are then not even the natural constituents of these "blobs"-cum-blocs—are considered and, for particular specifications, the monotonicity of world welfare examined, including even calculations concerning the "optimal" number of such symmetric PTAs/blocs! This, in turn, has led to critiques, as of the symmetry assumption by Srinivasan (1993), who essentially shows that the specific Krugman conclusions are easily reversed by abandoning symmetry, and to further variations by a few others.[52] Yet it is hard to see the analytical interest of this approach or, more important, its relevance to the compelling (incentive-structure) questions today concerning the membership expansion of PTAs. In short, it fails to throw light on the analysis of the dynamic time-path questions of the type introduced above. For that analysis, which is currently, quite correctly, on the top of the theoretical agenda, we must turn elsewhere.

Incentive Structure Arguments. At the April 1992 World Bank Conference on Regional Integration, Bhagwati (1993a), having reiterated the need to analyze the dynamic time-path question, advanced several arguments concerning the incentive structure within specific PTAs, once formed, to expand or to stagnate. Before we discuss the theoretical modeling of such ideas by Baldwin (1993), Krishna (1993), and Levy (1994), among others, it is worth recapitulating the principal arguments distinguished by Bhagwati.[53]

We need to recognize, of course, that the incentives may be political rather than (narrowly) economic. A PTA may be formed, and even expanded, to seek political allies by using trade as foreign policy and

---

52. See Deardorff and Stern (1994).

53. Bhagwati (1993a, 40–44) also discussed skeptically the claims that PTA formation is quicker, more efficient, and more certain than MTN.

to target the benefits of trade to politically favored nations.[54] Politics is not a negligible factor in the discriminatory trade arrangements implemented by the EU via Association Agreements with the smaller countries on its periphery and beyond; and it certainly cannot be ignored in the transformation of the original Canada-U.S. Free Trade Agreement into NAFTA with Mexico and then into the Enterprise of Americas Initiative.

But that is clearly not the whole story, and we can learn much by thinking carefully about the incentive structure for membership expansion in political-economy-theoretic terms. To do this, Bhagwati (1993a) distinguished among three different types of "agents" and offered the following analysis.

Governments of member countries. PTAs will be under pressure not to expand because governments may feel that "we already have a large market, so what do we stand to gain by going through the hassle of adding more members?" This is the "our market is large enough" syndrome, emphasized by Martin Wolf, who has often noted that large countries have tended to opt for inward-looking trade and investment strategies, while the small ones have gone the outward-looking route.

Interest groups in member countries. The interest groups in member countries may be for or against new members. The internationally oriented exporting firms may be expected to endorse new members whose markets then become preferentially available to them vis-à-vis nonmember exporters to these new members.[55] On the other hand, the firms that are profiting from access to preferential markets in the member (partner) countries will not want new members whose firms are also exporters of the same or similar products in the member markets. Both incentives reflect the preferential nature of the PTAs.

The former incentive was clear in the NAFTA debate in the United States and reflected in many pronouncements, including that of pro-

---

54. For an early analysis of the political factors underlying the formation of PTAs, see the work by the political scientist Edward Mansfield (1992) cited and discussed in Bhagwati (1993a). Other political scientists, such as Miles Kahler and Joseph Grieco, have written in this area recently.

55. In comparing incentives for export-oriented firms, for lobbying for a PTA (for example, NAFTA) as against MTN (for example, the Uruguay Round), a dollar's worth of lobbying would go a longer way in the former case because any preferential opening of the Mexican market would be better for the U.S. exporter than such an opening on an MFN basis that yields the benefits equally to U.S. rivals in Japan, the EU, and elsewhere. This argument applies only to the extent that the MTN process simultaneously does not open other markets to the U.S. exporter on a reciprocal basis.

NAFTA economists (and even President Clinton, who played the Japanophobic card that the United States would have preferential access to Mexico vis-à-vis Japan). It is also evident in the statement of Signor Agnelli of Fiat: "The single market must first offer an advantage to European companies. This is a message we must insist on without hesitation."

Interest groups in nonmember countries. The third set of agents is in the nonmember countries. Here the example of a PTA may lead others to emulate, even to seek, entry. Then again, the fear of trade diversion may also induce outsiders to seek entry.[56]

Recent Theoretical Analyses. Subsequently, the analysis of the dynamic time-path question moved into formal political economy–theoretic modeling. We provide here a synoptic review of the few significant contributions to date, organizing the literature analytically in light of the two questions distinguished above and also in terms of whether the analysis models the incentives of nonmembers to join or those of the members to expand.[57]

Question I. The single contribution that focuses on Question I (the incentive to add members to a PTA) is by Richard Baldwin (1993), who concentrates, in turn, on the incentive of nonmembers to join the PTA. He constructs a model to demonstrate that this incentive will be positive: the PTA will create a "domino" effect, with outsiders wanting to become insiders on an escalator. The argument is basically driven by

---

56. Bhagwati (1993a) cites Irwin's (1993) study of trade liberalization in the nineteenth century, which shows that the Anglo-French Treaty may well have served this purpose. Richard Baldwin's (1993) subsequent formalization of this basic idea in what he calls the "domino" theory of PTA expansion is discussed below.

57. In this review, we do not include the important contributions to the political economy–theoretic analysis of PTAs that do not directly address either of the two dynamic time-path questions at issue in the text. For example, Grossman and Helpman (1995) have modeled the formation of PTAs, demonstrating the critical role played by the possibility of trade diversion in the outcome, a conclusion also arrived at independently by Pravin Krishna (1995) in a different model. Similarly, Panagariya and Findlay (1996) have formalized the endogeneity argument that reduced protection between members in a PTA can lead to increased protection against nonmembers. Using a political process consisting of lobbying by owners of specific factors, they also investigate the external tariffs that emerge under an FTA and a CU. For answers to a similar set of questions, but under the assumption of a welfare-maximizing government, see our discussion of Bagwell and Staiger (1993).

the fact that the PTA implies a loss of cost competitiveness by imperfectly competitive nonmember firms whose profits in the PTA markets decline because they must face the tariffs that member countries' firms do not have to pay. These firms then lobby for entry, tilting the political equilibrium at the margin toward entry demands in their countries. The countries closest to the margin will then enter the bloc, assuming that the members have open entry. This enlarges the market and thereby increases the cost of nonmembership and pulls in countries at the next margin. Given the assumptions, including continuity, this domino model can take the PTA time-path to U^* in figure 1–9.

While Baldwin formalizes the incentive of nonmembers to get inside the PTA, interestingly there is no formalization of the incentives of members to add or reject new members that have been discussed in the literature, as by Bhagwati (1993a). Indeed, the Baldwin model itself shows, on the flip side, that member firms will gain from the cost advantage that they enjoy vis-à-vis the nonmember firms and hence will have an opposed interest in not admitting the nonmembers to the PTA: a full analysis of the political economy of both members and nonmembers in the Baldwin model could then lead to specific equilibrium outcomes that leave the PTA expansion imperiled.

Question II. The rest of the theoretical contributions address Question II, that is, whether the PTA possibility and/or time-path helps or harms the MTN time-path. Pravin Krishna (1993) and Philip Levy (1994) address directly and quite aptly this question and reach the "malign-impact" conclusion, unfavorable to the exhortation to "walk on both legs."

Krishna models the political process in the fashion of the government acting in response to implicit lobbying by firms, what Bhagwati (1990) has called a "clearinghouse"—government assumption where the government is passive, as in Findlay and Wellisz (1982). Krishna shows in his oligopolistic-competition model that the bilateral PTA between two member countries reduces the incentive of the member countries to liberalize tariffs reciprocally with the nonmember world and that, with sufficient trade diversion, this incentive could be so reduced as to make impossible an initially feasible multilateral trade liberalization.

Levy models the political process instead in a median-voter model à la Mayer (1984); the government is not what Bhagwati (1990) has called "self-willed" with its own objectives but acts again as a clearinghouse. Using a richer model with scale economies and product variety, Levy demonstrates that bilateral FTAs can undermine political support for multilateral free trade. At the same time, a benign impact is impossible in this model: if a multilateral free trade proposal is not feasible under autarky, the same multilateral proposal cannot be rendered feasible under any bilateral FTA.

The Krishna and Levy models throw light on the incentive-structure questions at hand when the agents are the lobbying groups and interests that are affected by different policy options. However, we might also note that there are contributions that take the more conventional view of governments, which act as agents maximizing social welfare (so that they may be regarded as acting as the custodians of the "general interest" as defined by economists), but then ask whether the effect of allowing PTAs to form affects outcomes concerning trade policy relating to the multilateral system. Rodney Ludema (1993) has analyzed the effect of PTAs on multilateral bargaining outcomes, arguing plausibly that the PTAs give strategic advantage to their members, whereas Kyle Bagwell and Robert Staiger (1993) have analyzed how the formation of a PTA—distinguishing between an FTA and a CU, as they yield different answers—will affect the (unbound) tariffs of the member countries on nonmembers.

The Sequential Bargaining Argument. In conclusion, we note that a different kind of model is implied, though not yet formalized, by the recent argument of Bhagwati (1994) that combines three separate notions.

The first is that even though a multilateral bargain *simultaneously* with a group of nonhegemonic powers is profitable and hence possible, a hegemonic power will gain a greater payoff by bargaining *sequentially* with them, using bilateral and plurilateral PTA approaches, picking the countries that are most vulnerable and then moving on to the next one and so on.[58]

The second is that this insight has now been appreciated by several lobbies (for example, the intellectual property protection lobby, the environmental and labor standard groups), which are piggybacking on to trade liberalization and trade institutions to secure their maximalist objectives and which see that the PTA approach (which may be seen as an "incentive" strategy), combined with the occasional use of aggressive unilateralism à la punitive Section 301 actions (which may

---

58. As noted in Bhagwati (1993a, 1994), this is exactly what the United States achieved, in terms of intellectual property protection and even concessions on environmental and labor standards enforcement, by getting then president Carlos Salinas into a one-on-one bargaining situation in NAFTA. And now Chile is poised to accept these obligations as the price of getting into NAFTA. On the other hand, as the virtually unanimous developing country objections to labor standards demands at the WTO show, neither Mexico nor Chile would have agreed to these demands in the purely WTO context.

be seen as a "punishment" strategy), is more likely to procure their objectives at the WTO and multilaterally than if pursued directly there through MTN alone.

The third is that the two processes, the MTN and the PTA paths, are to be traveled in tandem since the ultimate goal is indeed to arrive at multilateral, universal obligations in the areas desired by these lobbies by the nonhegemonic powers.

If this "model" provides insight into the political process driving the legitimation of the PTA time-path, then no hegemonic power is likely to abandon the PTA path simply because the WTO exists and is jumpstarted. A "selfish hegemon," looking after its own narrowly defined interests, reflecting its own lobbying-derived needs, will indeed want to "walk on both legs." But the multilateral outcome, so affected and determined, need not then be considered to have been affected in the socially optimal direction unless one makes the assumption, made effortlessly by hegemonic spokesmen in their policy pronouncements, that "what is good for the hegemon (and its lobbies) is good for the world trading system." Indeed, when we see that the intellectual property protections that were built into the WTO are almost certainly excessive according to the analytical and empirical argumentation of many of the best international economists today, it is hard to regard the ability of the hegemon to induce such outcomes with the aid of PTAs (and aggressive unilateralism) as creating a "benign" effect of the PTAs on the MTN path.

Implications for Current Policy

The case for PTAs, whether on static or on dynamic grounds, appears far less compelling and attractive than many politicians and policymakers now believe. In fact, it is likely that most of them, misled by the inevitable confusion between free trade and free trade areas that some economists have wittingly or unwittingly encouraged, are not even aware that the scholarly scene is rife today with serious opposition to PTAs.[59]

The Politics of PTAs. The current preoccupation with PTAs reflects

---

59. This was stated to be the case for Washington, D.C., by a well-placed trade economist in the Clinton administration, at a recent conference on the subject of PTAs. The first author, at a Stockholm conference on WTO issues in 1996, organized by the Swedish trade minister, Mats Hellström, found a similar unawareness among some of the trade ministers and bureaucrats present, even as the response of the attending economists to his critical remarks about the current obsession with PTAs was enthusiastic.

overriding political factors. Recall our earlier discussion of the sequen-
tial-bargaining advantage to hegemonic powers. Or consider the fact
that the leaders of the smaller, nonhegemonic powers get to play a
more prominent role, with better photo-opportunities, with smaller
summits, especially when a hegemonic power such as the United
States features its own president, than would ever be the case at the
WTO. Or consider that where the PTAs are regional, as is MERCOSUR
(among Argentina, Brazil, Paraguay, and Uruguay), the discriminatory
trade agreement can be depicted politically as an act of foreign policy
statesmanship. Or consider simply the operation of Gresham's Law:
PTAs by some encourage PTAs by others, especially when they are
being continually misportrayed by other politicians and countries as
statesmanlike moves to free trade. And, of course, there are always
the amateur geopoliticians and geoeconomists. Like little boys playing
Nintendo games on their computer screens, they think of playing the
game of "trade blocs" to indulge their pet prejudices against Europe
or Japan. Some want to make the APEC into a PTA to play off against
a "protectionist" Europe, while others think of TAFTA as a weapon to
play off against the "unfairly trading" Japan.[60]

The "Spaghetti Bowl" Phenomenon. Our view, for reasons explored
fully in this chapter, is that the spread of PTAs is desirable only when
two justifications obtain: you are building a Common Market with full-
scale integration of factor markets and even political harmonization; or
the multilateral MFN, MTN process is not working. As we argued earlier, neither rationale is operative today.

In fact, the proliferation of PTAs today poses the danger, indeed
the certainty, that a veritable "spaghetti bowl" phenomenon, as Bhagwati has called it, will emerge where trade barriers, including duties,
will vary depending on origin, and complex and protection-accommo-
dating rules of origin will find their way into practice.[61] And this, too,
at a time when multinationals are getting truly global, and the identi-
fication of "local content" and hence origin of traded goods and ser-

---

60. And then there are also those who think that the APEC, turned into a
PTA that excludes the extension of trade barrier reductions to Europe, will
prompt Europe to its own tariff cuts in a benign outcome. This viewpoint,
ascribed in the media to C. F. Bergsten, is premised on his view that the Seattle
APEC summit pushed the Europeans into settling the Uruguay Round. The
latter view is unpersuasive since, in the end, it was the U.S. administration that
decided to accept the advice of many to close the Round with whatever it
could get and to proceed to build on that in future negotiations. For a critique
of similar, special pleading to justify NAFTA, see Bhagwati (1995, 11–12).
61. For a detailed statement of this critique, see Bhagwati (1995).

vices is becoming increasingly meaningless and hence subject to inevitable arbitrariness. PTAs are just one, and indeed a gigantic, step backward from this reality: the need today is to intensify the commitment to the basic tenet of nondiscrimination that the architects of GATT correctly saw as a principal virtue, not to undermine it.

PTAs with and among Hegemons. We would therefore suggest that Article XXIV-sanctioned PTAs that involve hegemonic powers should be actively discouraged. They involve NAFTA extension southward or overseas, EU free-trade-area agreements with non-EU countries, APEC's transformation into a PTA, and TAFTA.

Such a self-denial would appear anti-free-trade, given the current state of confused thinking and the political capital invested by many in the cause of the PTAs. But it would be speaking to a far more compelling, and truer, version of free trade. It would also require true statesmanship on the part of the leaders of the hegemonic powers, as against the political advantages of opting for what is an inefficient and indeed harmful option.

PTAs among the Nonhegemons. Our view of PTAs among the nonhegemons, principally developing countries, is just a trifle less critical.

To begin with, what MERCOSUR does, for example, has only a fraction of the significance that the United States and the European Union have individually. The trade policy choices of the nonhegemons have comparatively more consequences for themselves than for the world. This contrast is sufficient to regard what they are doing with a less fiercely critical eye than that directed at the hegemons.

Remember again that the impact on their own welfare of PTAs is not necessarily benign. Especially, when these countries get into a PTA with hegemonic powers (for example, Mexico joining the United States in NAFTA), the outcomes for them may be welfare worsening (in the static sense) because of the tariff-revenue-redistribution effect, among other reasons. Failure to understand the differential economics of PTAs, as contrasted with that of free trade, underlies many of the favorable assessments often advanced in behalf of the developing countries that seek to join PTAs with the hegemonic powers.[62] A similar caveat

---

62. Unfortunately, this comment also applies to many of the numerical models, including the computable general-equilibrium models, estimating the gains from PTAs, as discussed by Panagariya in a forthcoming essay. And then there are the more elementary conceptual errors that afflict the numerical estimates of gains in *employment* from NAFTA. These errors were widely repeated by the media at the time.

would be relevant to PTAs among the nonhegemons themselves.

We may still consider these PTAs, such as MERCOSUR, with some favor, although nondiscriminatory free trade is the best option. After all, the acceptance of Article XXIV discipline (imperfect as it is) is an improvement over protectionism or over the utterly chaotic and arbitrary ECDC (economic cooperation among developing countries) at the GATT under which these countries were free from such discipline and could indulge in any level and kind of preferences among themselves.

Conclusion

At present, the spread of hegemonic PTAs has been halted. The Osaka meeting of APEC in November 1995 witnessed the Asian members of APEC reaffirming their desire to stick to MFN and hence implicitly to reject the PTA approach even though the U.S. position on the issue apparently remained problematic and ambiguous (with several pro-PTA proponents in the administration). Equally, at Madrid, the idea of TAFTA has been deflected away from an Article XXIV agreement to the New Trans-Atlantic Agenda that merely seeks, and in a presumably nondiscriminatory fashion, the lowering of trade and investment barriers in the area. For the time being, the extension of NAFTA to the South has also been halted, for reasons that may not hold for long beyond the presidential election in 1996.

All this yields enough time to take a closer look at the dangerous drift to PTAs that has been aided by the unfortunate conversion of the United States to the thesis that any trade liberalization is as good as any other. Perhaps, as often happens in economic policy, what presently looks like a politically irreversible trend will yield to economic wisdom. We will see.

Appendix A1: Varieties of PTAs
within the World Trade Organization

There are three categories of PTAs within the World Trade Organization framework. First, under Article XXIV, countries can form Free Trade Areas or Customs Unions. Of the one hundred thirty-four arrangements notified to the GATT/WTO as of June 1, 1995, 108 fell under this category (see table A1–1). Second, developing countries can form PTAs under the Enabling Clause. Here a full FTA or CU as defined in Article XXIV is not required, and partial preferences are allowed. Seventeen arrangements fall under this category. Finally, within the Generalized System of Preferences (GSP), a waiver from the MFN Article I may be given for preferences granted by developed countries to developing countries. Nine agreements fall under this category.

TABLE A1–1

134 REGIONAL TRADING ARRANGEMENTS NOTIFIED TO THE GATT/WTO, 1949–1995

Official Title	Usual Reference	Date of Entry into Force	GATT Cover
Interim Agreement for a Customs Union between the Union of South Africa and Southern Rhodesia	South Africa–South Rhodesia Customs Union	Apr. 1, 1949	Article XXIV
Free-Trade Treaty between the Republics of Nicaragua and El Salvador	El Salvador–Nicaragua Free Trade Area	Aug. 21, 1951	Article XXIV
Rome Treaty (European Economic Communities and European Atomic Energy Community)	EEC and EURATOM	Jan. 1, 1958	Article XXIV
Multilateral Central American Free Trade and Economic Integration Treaty (participation of Nicaragua)	Central American Free Trade Area	June 2, 1959	Article XXIV
Stockholm Convention (European Free Trade Association)	EFTA	May 3, 1960	Article XXIV
The Montevideo Treaty (Latin American Free Trade Area)	LAFTA	June 2, 1961	Article XXIV
Association of Finland with the European Free Trade Association	EFTA–Finland Association (FINEFTA)	June 26, 1961	Article XXIV

General Treaty for Central American Economic Integration (participation of Nicaragua)	Central American Common Market	Oct. 12, 1961	Article XXIV
The Borneo Free Trade Area	Borneo Free Trade Area	Jan. 1, 1962	Article XXIV
Trade Agreement between the Republic of Ghana and the Republic of Upper Volta	Ghana–Upper Volta Trade Agreement	May 9, 1962	Article XXIV
Regulation of Economic and Customs Relations between the Member States of the Equatorial Customs Union and the Federal Republic of Cameroon	Equatorial Customs Union—Cameroon Association	July 1, 1962	Article XXIV
Agreement setting up an association between the European Economic Community and Greece	EEC–Greece Association Agreement	Nov. 1, 1962	Article XXIV
African Common Market	African Common Market	June 1, 1963	Article XXIV
Convention of Association between the European Economic Community and the African and Malagasy States Associated with that community	Yaoundé I	Jan. 1, 1964	Article XXIV
Agreement for Economic Unity among Arab League States	Arab Common Market	Apr. 30, 1964	Article XXIV
Association between the EEC and certain non-European Countries and Territories maintaining special relations with France and the Netherlands, "PTOM-I"	EEC–PTOM I	June 1, 1964	Article XXIV

(table continues)

TABLE A1-1 (continued)

Official Title	Usual Reference	Date of Entry into Force	GATT Cover
Agreement creating an association between the European Economic Community and Turkey; "The Ankara Agreement"	EEC–Turkey Association Agreement of 1963	Dec. 1, 1964	Article XXIV
New Zealand/Australia Free Trade Agreement	Australia–New Zealand Free Trade Agreement	Jan. 1, 1966	Article XXIV
United Kingdom/Ireland Free Trade Area Agreement	Ireland–United Kingdom Free Trade Area	July 1, 1966	Article XXIV
Agreement Establishing the Caribbean Free Trade Association	CARIFTA	May 1, 1968	Article XXIV
Agreement establishing an association between the European Economic Community and the Kingdom of Morocco	EEC–Morocco Association Agreement of 1969	Sept. 1, 1969	Article XXIV
Agreement establishing an association between the European Economic Community and the Republic of Tunisia	EEC–Tunisia Association Agreement of 1969	Sept. 1, 1969	Article XXIV
European Free Trade Association; Accession of Iceland	EFTA/FINEFTA–Iceland Accession	Mar. 1, 1970	Article XXIV
Agreement between the European Economic Community and the State of Israel	EEC–Israel Agreement of 1970	Oct. 1, 1970	Article XXIV

Agreement between the European Economic Community and Spain	EEC–Spain Agreement of 1970	Oct. 1, 1970	Article XXIV
Agreement establishing an Association between the European Economic Community and the United Republic of Tanzania, the Republic of Uganda, and the Republic of Kenya	Arusha II Agreement	Jan. 1, 1971	Article XXIV
Association between the EEC and Certain Non-European Countries and Territories	EEC–PTOM II	Jan. 1, 1971	Article XXIV
EEC; African and Malagasy states and overseas countries and territories agreements	Yaoundé II	Jan. 1, 1971	Article XXIV
Agreement Establishing an Association between Malta and the European Economic Community	EEC–Malta Association Agreement	Apr. 1, 1971	Article XXIV
Agreements between Austria and the European Communities	EC–Austria Agreements of 1972	Oct. 1, 1972	Article XXIV
Treaty concerning the accession of the Kingdom of Denmark, Ireland, the Kingdom of Norway, and the United Kingdom of Great Britain and Northern Ireland	EC–Accession of Denmark, Ireland and United Kingdom	Jan. 1, 1973	Article XXIV
Agreements between the European Communities and Portugal	EC–Portugal Agreements of 1972	Jan. 1, 1973	Article XXIV

(table continues)

TABLE A1-1 (continued)

Official Title	Usual Reference	Date of Entry into Force	GATT Cover
Agreements between the European Communities and Sweden	EC–Sweden Agreements	Jan. 1, 1973	Article XXIV
Agreement between the European Economic Community and the Swiss Confederation	EC–Switzerland/ Liechtenstein Agreements	Jan. 1, 1973	Article XXIV
EEC; Turkey additional protocol to the Association Agreement	EEC–Turkey Additional Protocol to the Association Agreement	Jan. 1, 1973	Article XXIV
Agreement between the European Economic Community and the Republic of Iceland	EC–Iceland Agreements	Apr. 1, 1973	Article XXIV
Agreement between the European Economic Community and Cyprus	EEC–Cyprus Association Agreement	June 1, 1973	Article XXIV
Agreement between the European Economic Community and the Kingdom of Norway	EC–Norway Agreements	July 1, 1973	Article XXIV
Treaty establishing the Caribbean Community	CARICOM	Aug. 1, 1973	Article XXIV
Agreement between the European Economic Community and the Arab Republic of Egypt	EEC–Egypt Agreement of 1972	Nov. 1, 1973	Article XXIV

Agreement between the European Economic Community and the Lebanese Republic	EEC–Lebanon Agreement of 1972	Nov. 1, 1973	Article XXIV
Agreements between the European Communities and Finland	EC–Finland Agreements	Jan. 1, 1974	Article XXIV
Supplementary protocol to the Association Agreement between the European Economic Community and Turkey consequent on the accession of new member states to the Community	EC–Turkey Association Agreement of 1973	Jan. 1, 1974	Article XXIV
Agreement between the Republic of Finland and the People's Republic of Bulgaria on the reciprocal removal of obstacles to trade	Bulgaria–Finland Agreement	Jan. 1, 1975	Article XXIV
Agreement between the Republic of Finland and the Czechoslovak Socialist Republic on the reciprocal removal of obstacles to trade	Finland–Czechoslovakia Agreement	Jan. 1, 1975	Article XXIV
Agreement between the Republic of Finland and the Hungarian People's Republic on the reciprocal removal of obstacles to trade	Finland–Hungary Agreement	Jan. 1, 1975	Article XXIV
Additional protocol to the agreement establishing an association between the European Economic Community and Greece consequent on the accession of new member states to the Community	EEC–Greece Additional Protocol	July 1, 1975	Article XXIV

(table continues)

TABLE A1-1 (continued)

Official Title	Usual Reference	Date of Entry into Force	GATT Cover
Agreement between the European Economic Community and the State of Israel	EEC–Israel Agreement of 1975	July 1, 1975	Article XXIV
Agreement between the Republic of Finland and the German Democratic Republic on the removal of obstacles to trade on the basis of Reciprocity concerning advantages and obligations	Finland–German Democratic Republic Agreement	July 1, 1975	Article XXIV
ACP; EEC First Convention of Lomé	First Convention of Lomé	Apr. 1, 1976	Article XXIV
Interim agreement between the European Economic Community and the Peoples Democratic Republic of Algeria	EC–Algeria Agreements of 1976	July 1, 1976	Article XXIV
Interim agreement between the European Economic Community and the Kingdom of Morocco	EC–Morocco Agreements	July 1, 1976	Article XXIV
Interim agreement between the European Economic Community and the Republic of Tunisia	EC–Tunisia Agreements of 1976	July 1, 1976	Article XXIV
Interim agreement between the European Economic Community and the Portuguese Republic	EEC–Portugal Interim Agreement	Nov. 1, 1976	Article XXIV

Australia–Papua New Guinea Trade and Commercial Relations Agreement (PATCRA)	Australia–Papua New Guinea Agreement (PATCRA)	Feb. 1, 1977	Article XXIV
Interim cooperation agreement between the European Communities and the Arab Republic of Egypt	EEC–Egypt Interim Agreement of 1977	July 1, 1977	Article XXIV
Agreement between the European Economic Community and Jordan	EEC–Jordan Interim Agreement of 1977	July 1, 1977	Article XXIV
Agreement between the European Economic Community and Lebanon	EEC–Lebanon Interim Agreement of 1977	July 1, 1977	Article XXIV
Agreement between the European Economic Community and Syria	EEC–Syria Interim Agreement of 1977	July 1, 1977	Article XXIV
Agreement between the Republic of Finland and the Polish People's Republic on the reciprocal removal of obstacles to trade	Finland–Poland Agreement	Apr. 1, 1978	Article XXIV
EFTA–Spain Agreement	EFTA–Spain Agreement	May 1, 1980	Article XXIV
Interim agreement between the European Economic Community and the Socialist Federal Republic of Yugoslavia on trade and trade cooperation.	EEC–Yugoslavia Interim Agreement	July 1, 1980	Article XXIV
EEC–Greece Accession Agreement	EEC–Greece Accession Agreement	Jan. 1, 1981	Article XXIV

(table continues)

TABLE A1-1 (continued)

Official Title	Usual Reference	Date of Entry into Force	GATT Cover
ACP: EEC Second Convention of Lomé	Second Convention of Lomé	Jan. 1, 1981	Article XXIV
Australia–New Zealand Closer Economic Relations Trade Agreement (ANZCERTA)	Australia–New Zealand (ANZCERTA)	Jan. 1, 1983	Article XXIV
Agreement on the establishment of a free trade area between the Government of the United States of America and the Government of Israel	Israel–United States Free Trade Area Agreement	Aug. 19, 1985	Article XXIV
Accession of Portugal and Spain to the European Communities	EEC–Portugal and Spain Accessions	Jan. 1, 1986	Article XXIV
ACP: EEC Third Convention of Lomé	Third Convention of Lomé	Mar. 1, 1986	Article XXIV
Canada–United States Free Trade Agreement	Canada–U.S. Free Trade Agreement	Jan. 1, 1989	Article XXIV
Agreement between the European Community, of the one part, and the Government of Denmark and the Home Government of the Faroe Islands, of the other part	EC–Denmark and Faroe Islands Agreement	Jan. 1, 1992	Article XXIV

Interim agreement on trade and trade-related matters between the European Economic Community and the ECSC, of the one part, and the Czech and Slovak Federal Republic (CSFR), of the other part	EC–Czech and Slovak Federal Republic Interim Agreement of 1991	Mar. 1, 1992	Article XXIV
Interim agreement on trade and trade-related matters between the European Economic Community and the European Coal and Steel Community, of the one part, and Hungary, of the other part	EC–Hungary Interim Agreement of 1991	Mar. 1, 1992	Article XXIV
Interim agreement on trade and trade-related matters between the European Economic Community and the European Coal and Steel Community, of the one part, and Poland, of the other part	EC–Poland Interim Agreement of 1991	Mar. 1, 1992	Article XXIV
Agreement between the EFTA states and Turkey	EFTA–Turkey Agreement	Apr. 1, 1992	Article XXIV
Free trade agreement between the Kingdom of Norway and the Republic of Estonia	Estonia–Norway Free Trade Agreement	June 15, 1992	Article XXIV
Free trade agreement between the Kingdom of Norway and the Republic of Latvia	Latvia–Norway Free Trade Agreement	June 16, 1992	Article XXIV
Free trade agreement between the Kingdom of Norway and the Republic of Lithuania	Lithuania–Norway Free Trade Agreement	June 16, 1992	Article XXIV

(table continues)

TABLE A1-1 (continued)

Official Title	Usual Reference	Date of Entry into Force	GATT Cover
Agreement between the EFTA states and the Czech and Slovak Federal Republic	Czech and Slovak Federal Republic–EFTA Agreement	July 1, 1992	Article XXIV
Free trade agreement between the Kingdom of Sweden and the Republic of Estonia	Estonia–Sweden Free Trade Agreement	July 1, 1992	Article XXIV
Free trade agreement between the Kingdom of Sweden and the Republic of Estonia	Latvia–Sweden Free Trade Agreement	July 1, 1992	Article XXIV
Free trade agreement between the Kingdom of Sweden and the Republic of Lithuania	Lithuania–Sweden Free Trade Agreement	July 1, 1992	Article XXIV
Estonia–Finland protocol regarding temporary arrangements on trade and economic co-operation	Estonia–Finland Agreement	Dec. 1, 1992	Article XXIV
Czech Republic and Slovak Republic Customs Union	Czech Republic and Slovak Republic Customs Union	Jan. 1, 1993	Article XXIV
EFTA–Israel Free Trade Agreement	EFTA–Israel Free Trade Agreement	Jan. 1, 1993	Article XXIV

Central European Free Trade Agreement concluded by the Czech Republic, the Republic of Hungary, the Republic of Poland and the Slovak Republic	CEFTA	Mar. 1, 1993	Article XXIV
Free Trade Agreement between the Swiss Confederation and the Republic of Estonia	Estonia–Switzerland Free Trade Agreement	Apr. 1, 1993	Article XXIV
Free Trade Agreement between the Swiss Confederation and the Republic of Latvia	Latvia–Switzerland Free Trade Agreement	Apr. 1, 1993	Article XXIV
Free Trade Agreement between the Swiss Confederation and the Republic of Lithuania	Lithuania–Switzerland Free Trade Agreement	Apr. 1, 1993	Article XXIV
Interim agreement on trade and trade-related matters between the European Economic Community and the European Coal and Steel Community, of the one part, and Romania, of the other part	EEC–Romania Interim Agreement	May 1, 1993	Article XXIV
Agreement between the EFTA states and Romania	EFTA–Romania Agreement	May 1, 1993	Article XXIV
EFTA–Bulgaria Free Trade Agreement	EFTA–Bulgaria Free Trade Agreement	July 1, 1993	Article XXIV
Finland–Latvia protocol regarding temporary arrangements on trade and economic co-operation	Finland–Latvia Protocol	July 1, 1993	Article XXIV

(table continues)

67

TABLE A1-1 (continued)

Official Title	Usual Reference	Date of Entry into Force	GATT Cover
Finland–Lithuania Protocol regarding Temporary arrangements on trade and economic cooperation	Finland–Lithuania Protocol	July 1, 1993	Article XXIV
Cooperation agreement between the European Economic Community and the Republic of Slovenia	EEC–Slovenia Cooperation Agreement	July 19, 1993	Article XXIV
Agreement between the EFTA states and the Republic of Hungary	EFTA–Hungary Agreement	Oct. 1, 1993	Article XXIV
Agreement between the EFTA states and the Republic of Poland	EFTA–Poland Agreement	Nov. 15, 1993	Article XXIV
Interim agreement on trade and trade-related matters between the European Economic Community and the ECSC, of the one part, and the Republic of Bulgaria, of the other part	EEC–Bulgaria Interim Agreement	Dec. 31, 1993	Article XXIV
Free trade agreement between the Czech Republic and the Republic of Slovenia	Czech Republic–Slovenia Free Trade Agreement	Jan. 1, 1994	Article XXIV
North American Free Trade Agreement	NAFTA	Jan. 1, 1994	Article XXIV

Free trade agreement between the Slovak Republic and the Republic of Slovenia	Slovak Republic–Slovenia Free Trade Agreement	Jan. 1, 1994	Article XXIV
Austria, Finland, Sweden–EU accession agreement	Austria, Finland, Sweden–EU Accession Agreement	Jan. 1, 1995	Article XXIV
Czech Republic–Romania Free Trade Agreement	Czech Republic–Romania Free Trade Agreement	Jan. 1, 1995	Article XXIV
Agreement on free trade and trade-related matters between the European Community, the European Atomic Energy Community and the ECSC, of the one part, and the Republic of Estonia, of the other part	EC–Estonia Agreement	Jan. 1, 1995	Article XXIV
Agreement on free trade and trade-related matters between the European Community, the European Atomic Energy Community and the ECSC, of the one part, and the Republic of Latvia, of the other part	EC–Latvia Agreement	Jan. 1, 1995	Article XXIV
Agreement on free trade and trade-related matters between the European Community, the European Atomic Energy Community and the ECSC, of the one part, and the Republic of Lithuania, of the other part	EC–Lithuania Agreement	Jan. 1, 1995	Article XXIV

(table continues)

TABLE A1-1 (continued)

Official Title	Usual Reference	Date of Entry into Force	GATT Cover
Free trade agreement between the Republic of Hungary and the Republic of Slovenia	Hungary–Slovenia Free Trade Agreement	Jan. 1, 1995	Article XXIV
Slovak Republic–Romania Free Trade Agreement	Slovak Republic–Romania Free Trade Agreement	Jan. 1, 1995	Article XXIV
EFTA–Slovenia Free Trade Agreement	EFTA–Slovenia Free Trade Agreement	June 1, 1995	Article XXIV
The Unified Economic Agreement among the countries of the Gulf Cooperation Council	Gulf Cooperation Council		Enabling Clause
Additional protocol on preferential tariffs among members of the organization for economic co-operation (ECO)	Preferential Tariffs among ECO-members		Enabling Clause
South Asian Association for Regional Cooperation; Preferential Trade Arrangement (SAPTA)	SAPTA		Enabling Clause
Protocol relating to trade negotiations among developing countries	Protocol relating to Trade Negotiations among Developing Countries	Feb. 11, 1973	Enabling Clause

First agreement on trade negotiations among developing member countries of the Economic and Social Commission for Asia and the Pacific	Bangkok Agreement	June 17, 1976	Enabling Clause
Association of South-East Asian Nations ASEAN declaration	ASEAN Preferential Trading Arrangements	Aug. 31, 1977	Enabling Clause
South Pacific Regional Trade and Economic Cooperation Agreement	SPARTECA	Jan. 1, 1981	Enabling Clause
Second Treaty of Montevideo	Latin American Integration Association, "LAIA"	Mar. 18, 1981	Enabling Clause
Cartagena Agreement	Andean Group	May 25, 1988	Enabling Clause
Global System of Trade Preferences among developing countries (GSTP)	GSTP	Apr. 19, 1989	Enabling Clause
Trade agreement between the government of the Kingdom of Thailand and the government of the Lao People's Democratic Republic	Lao–Thailand Trade Agreement	June 20, 1991	Enabling Clause
Treaty of Asunción, Treaty Establishing a Common Market between the Argentine Republic, the Federal Republic of Brazil, the Republic of Paraguay, and the Eastern Republic of Uruguay	MERCOSUR	Nov. 29, 1991	Enabling Clause

(table continues)

TABLE A1-1 (continued)

Official Title	Usual Reference	Date of Entry into Force	GATT Cover
Common effective preferential tariff scheme for the ASEAN Free Trade Area	Preferential Tariff Scheme for the ASEAN Free Trade Area	Jan. 28, 1992	Enabling Clause
Common Market for Eastern and Southern Africa	COMESA	Dec. 8, 1994	Enabling Clause
Bolivia–Mexico Free Trade Treaty	Bolivia–Mexico Free Trade Treaty	Jan. 1, 1995	Enabling Clause
Mexico–Costa Rica Free Trade Area	Mexico–Costa Rica Free Trade Area	Jan. 1, 1995	Enabling Clause
Colombia, Mexico, and Venezuela Free Trade Agreement	Treaty of the Group of Three (G3)	Jan. 1, 1995	Enabling Clause
Australian treatment of products of Papua New Guinea	Australian Treatment of Products of Papua New Guinea		Waiver–Art. I:1
French trading arrangements with Morocco	France–Morocco Trading Arrangements		Waiver–Art. I:1
	Australia–Federation of Rhodesia and Nyasaland Agreement	July 1, 1955	Waiver–Art. I:1

United States Caribbean Basin Economic Recovery Act	U.S.–Caribbean CBERA	Jan. 1, 1984	Waiver–Art. I:1
Canadian tariff treatment for commonwealth Caribbean countries	CARIBCAN	May 12, 1986	Waiver–Art. I:1
ACP—EEC Fourth Convention of Lomé	Fourth Convention of Lomé	Sept. 1, 1991	Waiver–Art. I:1
Andean Trade Preference Act	U.S.–Andean Trade Preference Act	Dec. 4, 1991	Waiver–Art. I:1
Trade agreement between the governments of the Federation of Rhodesia and Nyasaland and the Union of South Africa	Federation of Rhodesia/Nyasaland–South Africa Agreement of 1955	July 1, 1955	Waiver–Art. I:2
	Federation of Rhodesia/Nyasaland–South Africa Agreement of 1960	July 1, 1960	Waiver–Art. I:2

References

Bagwell, Kyle, and Robert Staiger. "Multilateral Cooperation During the Formation of Free Trade Areas." NBER Working Paper no. 4364, 1993.

Baldwin, Richard. "A Domino Theory of Regionalism." CEPR Working Paper no. 857, November 1993.

Berglas, Eitan. "Preferential Trading: The n Commodity Case." *Journal of Political Economy*, vol. 87, 1979, pp. 315–31.

Bhagwati, Jagdish. "Trade Liberalization Among LDCs, Trade Theory and GATT Rules." In J. N. Wolf, ed., *Value, Capital, and Growth: Papers in Honour of J. R. Hicks.* Oxford: Oxford University Press, 1968.

———. "The Theory of Political Economy, Economic Policy, and Foreign Investment." In M. Scott and D. Lal, eds., *Public Policy and Economic Development*, Essays in Honor of I.M.D. Little, pp. 217–30. Oxford: Clarendon Press, 1990.

———. *The World Trading System at Risk.* Princeton, N.J.: Princeton University and Harvester Wheatsheaf, 1991.

———. "Regionalism and Multilateralism: An Overview." In Jaime de Melo and Arvind Panagariya, eds., *New Dimensions in Regional Integration.* Cambridge: Cambridge University Press, 1993a.

———. "Beyond NAFTA: Clinton's Trading Choices." *Foreign Policy*, Summer 1993b, pp. 155–62.

———. "Threats to the World Trading System: Income Distribution and the Selfish Hegemon." *Journal of International Affairs*, vol. 48, Spring 1994, pp. 279–85.

———. "U.S. Trade Policy: The Infatuation with Free Trade Areas." In Jagdish Bhagwati and Anne O. Krueger, *The Dangerous Drift to Preferential Trade Agreements.* Washington, D.C.: AEI Press, 1995.

———. "Trade and Wages: A Malign Relationship?" In Susan Collins, ed., *The American Worker: Exports, Imports and Jobs.* Washington, D.C.: Brookings Institution, forthcoming (1996a).

———. "Watering of Trade." *Journal of International Economics*, forthcoming (1996b).

Bhagwati, Jagdish, and Vivek Dehejia. "Trade and Wages: Is Marx Striking Again?" In Jagdish Bhagwati and M. Kosters, eds., *Trade and Wages: Leveling Wages Down?* Washington, D.C.: AEI Press, 1994.

Bhagwati, Jagdish, Pravin Krishna, and Arvind Panagariya. "Introduction." In Jagdish Bhagwati and Pravin Krishna, eds., *Contributions to the Theory of Preferential Trading Areas.* Cambridge, Mass.: MIT Press, forthcoming.

Bhagwati, Jagdish, and Arvind Panagariya. "The Theory of Preferential Trade Agreements: Historical Evolution and Current Trends." *American Economic Review*, vol. 86, pp. 82–87.

Bhagwati, Jagdish, and T. N. Srinivasan. "Revenue Seeking: A Generalization of the Theory of Tariffs." *Journal of Political Economy*, vol. 88, December 1980, pp. 1069–87.

———. *Lectures in Trade Theory*. Cambridge, Mass.: MIT Press, 1983.

Bliss, Christopher. *Economic Theory and Policy for Trading Blocs*. Manchester and New York: Manchester University Press, 1994.

Brecher, Richard, and Jagdish Bhagwati. "Foreign Ownership and the Theory of Trade and Welfare." *Journal of Political Economy*, vol. 89, June 1981, pp. 497–511.

Cooper, C. A., and B. F. Massell. "A New Look at Customs Union Theory." *Economic Journal*, vol. 75, 1965a, pp. 742–47.

———. "Towards a General Theory of Customs Unions for Developing Countries." *Journal of Political Economy*, vol. 73, 1965b, pp. 461–76.

Deardorff, Alan V., and Robert M. Stern. "Multilateral Trade Negotiations and Preferential Trading Arrangements." In Alan V. Deardorff and Robert M. Stern, eds., *Analytical and Negotiating Issues in the Global Trading System*. Ann Arbor: University of Michigan Press, 1994.

de Melo, Jaime, and Arvind Panagariya, ed. *New Dimensions in Regional Integration*. Cambridge, Great Britain: Cambridge University Press, 1993.

de Melo, Jaime, Arvind Panagariya, and Dani Rodrik. "The New Regionalism: A Country Perspective." In Jaime de Melo and Arvind Panagariya, eds., *New Dimensions in Regional Integration*, chap. 6. Cambridge, Great Britain: Cambridge University Press, 1993.

Dhar, Sumana, and Arvind Panagariya. "Is East Asia Less Open than North America and the European Economic Community? No." Policy Research Working Paper no. 1370. Washington, D.C.: World Bank, 1994.

Eaton, Jonathan, and Arvind Panagariya. "Gains from Trade under Variable Returns to Scale, Commodity Taxation, Tariffs and Factor Market Distortions." *Journal of International Economics*, vol. 9, 1979, pp. 481–501.

Findlay, Ronald, and Stanislaw Wellisz. "Endogenous Tariffs, the Political Economy of Trade Restrictions and Welfare." In Jagdish Bhagwati, ed., *Import Competition and Response*. Chicago and London: University of Chicago Press, 1982.

Frankel, Jeffrey, and Sheng-Jin Wei. "The New Regionalism and Asia: Impact and Options." Paper presented at the Asian Development Bank Conference on Emerging Global Trading Environment and Developing Asia, May 29–30, 1995.

Frankel, Jeffrey, E. Stein, and Shing-Jin Wei. "Trading Blocs and the Americas: The Natural, the Unnatural and the Supernatural." *Journal of Development Economics*, vol. 47, June 1995a, pp. 61–96.

———. "Continental Trading Blocs: Are They Natural or Super-Natural?" NBER Working Paper no. 4588, 1995b.

Grossman, Gene, and Elhanan Helpman. "The Politics of Free Trade Agreements." *American Economic Review*, September 1995, pp. 667–90.

Haberler, Gottfried. "The Political Economy of Regional or Continental Blocs." In Seymour. E. Harris, ed., *Postwar Economic Problems*. New York. 1943.

Irwin, Douglas. "Multilateral and Bilateral Trade Policies in the World Trading System: An Historical Perspective." In Jaime de Melo and Arvind Panagariya, eds., *New Dimensions in Regional Integration*. Cambridge, Great Britain: Cambridge University Press, 1993.

Johnson, Harry. *Money, Trade and Economic Growth*. Cambridge, Mass.: Harvard University Press, 1962.

———. "An Economic Theory of Protectionism, Tariff Bargaining, and the Formation of Customs Unions." *Journal of Political Economy*, vol. 73, June 1965, pp. 256–83.

Kemp, Murray C., and Henry Wan. "An Elementary Proposition Concerning the Formation of Customs Unions." *Journal of International Economics*, vol. 6, February 1976, pp. 95–98.

Krishna, Pravin. "Regionalism and Multilateralism: A Political Economy Approach." Economics Department, Columbia University, mimeo, December 1993. Presented to the NBER Universities Research Conference on International Trade and Regulations, Cambridge, Mass., 1993.

Krishna, Pravin, and Jagdish Bhagwati. "Necessarily Welfare-Enhancing Customs Unions with Industrialization Constraints: A Proof of the Cooper-Massell-Johnson-Bhagwati Conjecture." Columbia University Working Papers, April 1994.

Krueger, Anne O. "The Political-Economy of the Rent Seeking Society." *American Economic Review*, vol. 69, 1974, pp. 291–303.

———. "Rules of Origin as Protectionist Devices." NBER Working Paper no. 4352, April 1993. [Forthcoming] in J. Melvin, J. Moore, and R. Riezman, eds. *International Trade Theory: Essays in Honour of John Chipman*. United Kingdom: Routledge, 1996.

———. "Free Trade Agreements versus Customs Unions." NBER Working Paper no. 5084, April 1995.

Krugman, Paul. "The Move to Free Trade Zones." In Symposium sponsored by the Federal Reserve Bank of Kansas City, *Policy Implications of Trade and Currency Zones*, 1991a.

———. "Is Bilateralism Bad?" In E. Helpman and A. Razin, eds., *International Trade and Trade Policy*. Cambridge, Mass.: MIT Press, 1991b.

———. "Regionalism versus Multilateralism: Analytical Notes." In Jaime de Melo and Arvind Panagariya, eds., *New Dimensions in Re-*

gional Integration. Cambridge, Great Britain: Cambridge University Press, 1993.

Lawrence, Robert Z. "Emerging Regional Arrangements: Building Blocks or Stumbling Blocks?" In Richard O'Brien, ed., *Finance and the International Economy*, Amex Bank Prize Essays. Oxford: Oxford University Press for the Amex Bank Review, 1991.

Levy, Philip. "A Political Economic Analysis of Free Trade Agreements." *American Economic Review*, forthcoming.

Lipsey, Richard. "The Theory of Customs Unions: Trade Diversion and Welfare." *Economica*, vol. 24, 1957, pp. 40–46.

———. *The Theory of Customs Unions: A General Equilibrium Analysis*. University of London, Ph.D. thesis, 1958.

———. "The Theory of Customs Unions: A General Survey." *Economic Journal*, vol. 70, 1960, pp. 498–513.

Lloyd, Peter J. "3×3 Theory of Customs Unions." *Journal of International Economics*, vol. 12, 1982, pp. 41–63.

Ludema, Rodney. "On the Value of Preferential Trade Agreements in Multilateral Negotiations." Mimeo. 1993.

Mansfield, Edward. "The Concentration of Capabilities and International Trade." *International Organization*.

Mayer, Wolfgang. "Endogenous Tariff Formation." *American Economic Review*, vol. 74, December 1984, pp. 970–85.

Meade, James E. *The Theory of Customs Unions*. Amsterdam: North-Holland, 1955.

Mundell, Robert A. "Tariff Preferences and the Terms of Trade." *Manchester School of Economic and Social Studies*, vol. 32, 1964, pp. 1–13.

Panagariya, Arvind. "Should East Asia Go Regional? No, No and Maybe." WPS 1209. Washington, D.C.: World Bank, 1993.

———. "East Asia and the New Regionalism." *World Economy*, vol. 17, November 1994, pp. 817–39.

———. "Rethinking the New Regionalism." Paper presented at the Trade Expansion Program Conference of the United Nations Development Programme and World Bank, January 1995a.

———. "The Free Trade Area of the Americas: Good for Latin America?" Working Paper no. 12, *World Economy*, forthcoming. Center for International Economics, University of Maryland, 1995.

———. "Preferential Trading and the Myth of Natural Trading Partners." Working Paper no. 200, Center for Japan-U.S. Business and Economic Studies, Stern School of Business, New York University, New York, 1996a.

———. "The Meade Model of Preferential Trading: History, Analytics and Policy Implications." Mimeo, University of Maryland, Department of Economics, 1996b.

Panagariya, Arvind, and Ronald Findlay. "A Political Economy Analysis of Free Trade Areas and Customs Unions." In Robert Feenstra, Gene Grossman, and Douglas Irwin, eds., *The Political Economy of Trade Reform*, Essays in Honor of Jagdish Bhagwati. Cambridge, Mass.: MIT Press, 1996.

Polak, Jacques J. "Is APEC a Natural Regional Trading Bloc? A critique of the 'Gravity Model' of International Trade." Mimeo (revised version to appear in the *World Economy*).

Richardson, M. "Why a Free Trade Area? The Tariff Also Rises." *Economics & Politics*, vol. 6, March 1994, pp. 79–95.

Riezman, Raymond. "A 3×3 Model of Customs Unions." *Journal of International Economics*, vol. 9, 1979, pp. 341–54.

Srinivasan, T. N. "Discussion." In Jaime de Melo and Arvind Panagariya, eds., *New Dimensions in Regional Integration*. Cambridge, Great Britain: Cambridge University Press, 1993.

———. "Common External Tariffs of a Customs Union: The Case of Identical Cobb-Douglas Tastes." Mimeo, Yale University, 1995.

Summers, Lawrence. "Regionalism and the World Trading System." Symposium Sponsored by the Federal Reserve Bank of Kansas City, *Policy Implications of Trade and Currency Zones*, 1991.

Viner, Jacob. *The Customs Union Issue*. New York: Carnegie Endowment for International Peace, 1950.

Wei, Sheng-Jin, and Jeffrey Frankel. "Open Regionalism in a World of Continental Trade Blocs." Revised version of NBER Working Paper no. 5272, November 1995.

Winters, L. A. "Regionalism and the Rest of the World: The Irrelevance of the Kemp-Wan Theorem." Mimeo. Washington, D.C.: World Bank, 1995a.

———. "European Integration and Economic Welfare in the Rest of the World." Mimeo. Washington, D.C.: World Bank, 1995b.

Wolf, Martin. "Comments." In Jeffrey J. Schott, ed., *Free Trade Areas and U.S. Trade Policy*, pp. 89–95. Washington, D.C.: Institute for International Economics, 1989.

Wonnacott, Paul, and Mark Lutz. "Is There a Case for Free Trade Areas?" In Schott, Jeffrey J., ed., *Free Trade Areas and U.S. Trade Policy*, pp. 59–84. Washington, D.C.: Institute for International Economics, 1989.

2
Beyond NAFTA—The Design of a Free Trade Agreement of the Americas

Paul Wonnacott

In 1990, President Bush enunciated his Enterprise for the Americas Initiative, outlining his vision of a hemisphere-wide free trade arrangement running from Alaska and the Northwest Territories to Tierra del Fuego. In December 1994, at the Summit of the Americas in Miami, President Clinton and other hemispheric heads of state reiterated and reinforced this vision, declaring their commitment to a hemisphere-wide free trade agreement by the year 2005.

This chapter will address some of the questions facing the nations of the Americas as they move toward a free trade agreement (FTA). In particular, I will look at the institutional arrangements that might be used as a basis for a Free Trade Association of the Americas (FTAA). Specifically, I will consider several closely related topics:

- Overlapping FTAs: that is, "hub-and-spoke" arrangements and more complex variants. What are the implications of overlapping FTAs for efficiency? Why are overlapping free-trade agreements negotiated? What could or should be done to deal with the inefficiencies that arise when there are overlapping FTAs?
- Problems that arise from rules of origin in an FTA. What, if anything, can be done to reduce the onerous administrative burdens that they impose on exporters?
- Comparative merits of FTAs and Customs Unions (CUs) and the possibility of intermediate arrangements, such as were foreshadowed in the NAFTA agreement on computers, where there will be a "match-

For their comments and suggestions, I am indebted to Gary Hufbauer, Arvind Panagariya, Ronald Wonnacott, and the participants in the Conference on Capital Flows and Regionalism, Center for International Economics, University of Maryland and American Enterprise Institute, June 13, 1995.

ing external tariff"—in effect, a common external tariff (CET)—moving to zero and allowing an elimination of rules of origin.

- Rules of accession.
- An FTAA and other free-trade proposals.

To summarize my main conclusion, I will suggest a hybrid system between an FTA and a customs union.[1] In general, the rules would be the same as with a customs union for some products: a common external tariff and no rules of origin. For other products, FTA rules would apply: members would maintain independent tariffs on imports from outside countries and would also maintain rules of origin on those products. The hybrid arrangement would be different from a standard FTA in a number of respects:

- For some products, it would eliminate the burdens associated with rules of origin.

- *Provided that the common external tariff were greater than zero on at least some products,* the hybrid arrangement would require agreement of current members before new members were included, and it would prevent current members from entering independent FTAs with outside countries. That is, it would limit the freedom of any FTAA member to strike independent deals with outside members. The reason is that, in agreeing to the CET on some products, individual members would give up their independent right to eliminate the CET on imports from countries outside the FTAA. Thus, the existence of some CET would not only reduce the rule of origin problem, but would also prevent the proliferation of hub-and-spokes or more complex overlapping arrangements.

- A hybrid system would require tighter cooperation than a regular FTA because agreement would have to be reached on the CET in some products. It would not require nearly such tight cooperation as a CU, however, because countries would retain their right to set independent tariffs on third-country imports for other products. The most difficult products—those on which attitudes differ substantially among members—would presumably be the ones on which individual members would maintain their individual external tariffs. The CET would apply to the easier cases on which agreement could be reached more readily.

The core of this chapter—starting in the section on free trade with Mexico—will deal with the complexities that can arise when more than two countries discuss free trade arrangements. This discussion begins

---

1. This chapter draws on earlier work of Ronald Wonnacott and on our earlier joint work, most notably, Wonnacott and Wonnacott (1995) and R. J. Wonnacott (1975a).

with the question posed in 1990, of how the prospective Mexican-U.S. free trade agreement would be related to the earlier U.S.-Canadian free trade agreement. But first, I summarize the history of U.S.-Canadian relations and U.S.-Canadian free trade.

The Historical Background to NAFTA

Accidents of history and geography have made the economic and political relations between the United States and Canada unique. Coming largely from European stock, Americans and Canadians are similar in many respects. They are different, however, in ways that to Americans seem subtle but to Canadians, centrally important. Americans often say that Canadians are just like them—an observation meant as a good-natured compliment but rarely taken as such. Most Canadians live within a hundred miles of the United States and often feel overwhelmed by the flood of communications bubbling over the border, most notably through television and radio. In defining their nationality, Canadians focus precisely on the ways in which they are different from Americans. One is a difference in attitudes toward government: the United States is founded on the ideals of inalienable individual rights and the pursuit of happiness; Canada, on the idea of stability and good government. Compared with the U.S. government, the Canadian government commands greater trust and respect among its people and has played a greater role in the economy: the building of the Canadian National Railways early in the century, the establishment of the government-owned Canadian Broadcasting Corporation, and, more recently, the single-payer government medical program and tight control on handguns.

Not surprisingly, Americans and Canadians have historically had quite different attitudes toward the American Revolution. Particularly in the early days, Americans rather assumed that Canadians would, if offered the opportunity, join the United States. This expectation led to disappointing American military operations on Canadian soil, first with the abortive attack on Quebec City on New Year's Eve 1775 and later during the War of 1812. The first large-scale English-speaking immigration into Ontario consisted of refugees from the American Revolution—"Tories" to Americans but "United Empire Loyalists" to Canadians. Historically, Canadians looked on the American Revolution more with sorrow than with anger: sorrow that the English-speaking world had been shattered so needlessly, and sorrow that blood had been spilled even though it was inevitable that America's relative power would grow and de facto independence evolve even in the absence of military conflict. This preference for evolution as contrasted to military solutions has lasted to the current day. When America had its constitutional crisis over a century ago, it led to the Civil War. Canada has been going through a prolonged constitutional crisis over the past two decades, but it is unthinkable that the Quebecois, if they should decide to separate through a clear and unambiguous vote, would be kept within confederation by force of arms.

The American Revolution left the North American continent divided. But the very practical question remained of the economic relations between the United States and "British North America." Much of Canadian trade was with Britain, where Canadian goods were granted preferential access because they originated within the empire. But for many Canadian businesses seeking to expand beyond their local markets, the most obvious customers lay to the south, across the U.S. border. With most of the Canadian population stretched in a narrow, 100-mile-wide, 3,000-mile-long ribbon hugging the U.S. border, many of the closest, most promising markets were in the United States. The ties to the south were particularly strong because the population ribbon is interrupted in midcontinent. The central Canadian shield of rock, dominating the thousand miles from Toronto to Winnipeg, is utterly inhospitable to farming, although dotted with rich bodies of ore and an occasional port. Surface communications between eastern and western Canada lie naturally through the Great Lakes or through the United States, not through northern Ontario.

Thus began the central economic drama of Canadian history: to what extent would the natural north-south economic ties be allowed to dominate, and to what extent would they be overridden by government policies aimed at tying Canada together with east-west trade and communications?

One of the early scenes in this drama began when the British moved toward unilateral free trade in the middle of the nineteenth century with the repeal of the Corn Laws. No longer did Canadian exports enjoy substantial preferences as they entered Britain. Feeling forsaken by the empire, Canadians responded in two ways. One was a "tit-for-tat." British preferences in the Canadian market were almost eliminated by an increase in Canadian tariffs on British goods and a cut in tariffs on U.S. goods. The second response was sharper—to move toward even closer ties with the United States than with Britain. Many of the Scottish business elite of Montreal joined the Annexation Movement of 1849, aimed at outright union with the United States. Less drastically, overtures were made for free trade with the United States. In 1854, the Reciprocity Treaty provided for free trade in natural products between the Canadian provinces and the United States. The

United States quickly replaced Britain as Canada's principal trading partner.

Relations between Britain and the United States soured, however, because of British sympathy with the South in the Civil War. The United States took out its resentments on Canada, abrogating the Reciprocity Treaty in 1866. Forsaken by Britain and rebuffed by the United States, the Canadian provinces looked to one another, joining in confederation in 1867.

But the U.S. market still beckoned, and the Canadian government quickly negotiated a new reciprocity treaty. It died in the U.S. Senate. The pendulum then swung in the other direction, with the Conservative government's National Policy of protection, aimed at stimulating east-west trade within Canada. But even this strongly protectionist move reflected an ambivalence: perhaps Canadian tariffs could be used as a bargaining lever. Prime Minister Macdonald argued that "it is only by closing our doors . . . that they will open theirs to us."[2]

Once again the pendulum swung. Canada again approached the United States in the late 1880s about reciprocity and was once again rebuffed. Secretary of State James Blaine bluntly announced that he was "opposed, teetotally opposed, to giving the Canadians the sentimental satisfaction of waving the British flag . . . and enjoying . . . American markets. They cannot have both" (Waite 1971, 223). But Canadians *could* have had it both ways, if they had so chosen. A new reciprocity treaty was negotiated in 1911, providing for free trade in natural products and lower tariffs on manufactures. But it, and its Liberal Party negotiators, could not withstand the nonsensical but powerful rallying cry of opponents, "No truck nor trade with the Yankees." Both went down to defeat in the election of 1911. Free trade, however, proved to be the issue that would not die in Canadian politics. Shortly after World War II, the two countries drafted a secret free trade agreement. Although Prime Minister Mackenzie King had approved the negotiations, his caution led him to scuttle it.

During the 1970s and early 1980s, conditions ripened for a free trade agreement. The success of the European Community led some in the United States to consider regional arrangements more favorably. And it left Canadian businesses feeling at a disadvantage, having un-

---

2. *Debates, House of Commons*, March 7, 1878, as quoted by Granatstein (1985, 17). This theme was repeated a half-century later, by Conservative leader R. B. Bennett in his campaign to become prime minister. He told his audience that he would use higher Canadian tariffs "to blast a way into the markets that have been closed to you" (as quoted by Colombo 1974).

restricted access to only the small Canadian market. In the words of one senior Canadian executive:

> We, manufacturers, are caught in a Catch-22 situation. On the one hand, the tariffs in Canada are no longer high enough to offset the higher costs of producing solely for the Canadian market. On the other hand, even modest tariffs into the US can make it difficult, if not impossible, to set up production in Canada to export into that market.[3]

The peculiar problem of Canadian manufacturing—producing for a small market that was exposed to U.S. advertising and wanted a broad choice of products—attracted considerable academic attention (English 1964; Eastman and Stykolt 1967; Wonnacott and Wonnacott 1967; Spence 1977, 1980; Harris and Cox 1984). A central problem was how to get economies of scale. The best hope lay in the export market, and that meant primarily the U.S. market, since about three-fifths of Canadian exports went to the United States. The Auto Pact of 1965 illustrated the advantages of tariff-free trade between the two countries; Canadian plants were able to specialize on a few models, with much of their output being sent to the United States in exchange for models not produced in Canada. Between 1965 and 1985, there was a revolution in Canadian business attitudes toward free trade with the United States; it was increasingly seen as the best hope for becoming competitive in the world economy.

Ultimately, however, fear proved a stronger motive than hope in pushing the Mulroney government to request free trade talks in 1985. With the soaring U.S. dollar and increasing U.S. trade deficits, protectionist measures were being seriously considered by the U.S. Congress. Canadian business was increasingly concerned with the U.S. use of antidumping and, especially, countervailing duties—measures that Americans identified as "trade remedy laws" but Canadians labeled "contingent protection." Canada had four main objectives in the negotiations: to insulate itself from a possible swing toward protection in the United States, to negotiate the phasing out of tariffs to gain even greater access to U.S. markets, to maintain a degree of protection for Canadian cultural industries, and to negotiate a disputes settlements agreement that would give Canada some insulation from what it considered an arbitrary application of U.S. trade remedy laws.[4] In the final

---

3. J. E. Newall, chairman, DuPont Canada, as quoted in Royal Commission 1985, 300.

4. Canadians were particularly concerned about the reversal of the U.S. government on lumber, which seemed to them to be a politically inspired application of the countervailing duty law. In 1983, Canadian stumpage fees were

stages of the negotiation, the inclusion of a disputes settlements clause became a sine qua non for Canada.

With the opening of U.S.-Canadian negotiations, some Americans, particularly in the southern states, began to look seriously at the possibility of free trade with Mexico. Governor Jerry Brown of California, for example, sponsored a conference on that topic. Free trade with Mexico would in some respects be quite different from that with Canada; unlike Canada, Mexico had a much lower standard of living than the United States, and there was much less cultural affinity between the two countries. If, before World War I, Canadians responded to the cry of "No truck nor trade with the Yankees," Mexican attitudes were summed up in the caustic observation of President Diaz: "Poor Mexico! So far from God, and so close to the United States."

As in the U.S.-Canadian case, it was not so much changes in U.S. attitudes as changes in the smaller partner that led to U.S.-Mexican free trade negotiations. Because of the overwhelming size of the U.S. economy compared with the economies of other Western Hemisphere countries, it has always been important that any specific initiative for a free trade agreement come from the other countries, not from the United States. Thus, it was Canadian Prime Minister Mulroney who took the initiative in requesting bilateral free trade negotiations with the United States. The stakes in a bilateral FTA were so much greater for Canada than for the United States, in risks, adjustment costs, and potential gains, including gains from economies of scale. Therefore, it was essential that the initiative be seen as coming from Canada, and being in Canada's interest, and not—as opponents would surely charge[5]—representing an extension of American "economic imperial-

---

found by the U.S. government not to represent countervailable subsidies, but this decision was reversed in 1986 even though the facts were essentially unchanged.

On the other side, Americans were concerned with the propensity of the Canadian government to tinker in the economy, which resulted, in part, from the greater trust of Canadians in their government. Some Americans considered the secret duty rebates offered to Japanese auto firms in Canada to verge on bad faith.

On these two issues, see Wonnacott (1987), chap. 4. The heat generated over trade remedy laws and other trade disputes (such as the beer case) should not obscure the fact that the vast bulk of U.S.-Canadian trade takes place quietly, without controversy or fanfare.

5. For example, Shirley Carr, president of the Canadian Labour Congress, attacked the free-trade negotiations:

It is in the interest of the United States to try to take over Canada. It has always been, ever since Canada was first formed. . . . They want ism." Similarly, the negotiations for free trade between the United States and Mexico came at Mexican request—a request that, in Robert Pastor's words (1995), "shattered a national tradition." The negotiations with Chile are likewise at Chile's request.[6]

These Latin American initiatives result from a revolution in attitudes toward trade and markets. The 1960s, 1970s, and 1980s provided one of the clearest, least ambiguous lessons of economic history: the Latin strategy of import substitution was inferior to East Asian export-oriented policies. This lesson led to strong unilateral steps toward freer trade, notably in Chile, and to the Mexican decision to enter the General Agreement on Tariffs and Trade (GATT). The stage was set for the Mexican approach to the United States in early 1990, requesting free trade talks.

Charges of gringo imperialism are less dangerous now, with the healthy changes in attitude that are taking place in both Latin America *and* the United States, away from the idea of Latin America as a set of client states to which the United States may from time to time grant crumbs, and toward the idea that the international market is a place to do serious business, for the mutual benefit of all countries. But it still remains important that Latin American countries see any participation in an FTA as their initiative, undertaken in their own interests, and not as a grandiose scheme foisted on them by Washington. If we move toward the sort of hybrid FTA suggested in this chapter, with its greater coordination of tariffs, the importance of initiatives coming from the Latin countries will be enhanced.[7]

---

to disrupt and disturb everything we have and bring us down to their level. [Interview reported by the Canadian Press, Aug. 17, 1986.]

It may seem strange that labor unions on both sides of the border have generally been negative on free trade initiatives. Although free trade might in theory adversely affect a country, it is hard to imagine how it could make all countries worse off. But there is a possible explanation for the international opposition of labor unions to free trade. Even though free trade increases efficiency and generally raises living standards and wage rates, it increases competition and increases the elasticity of demand for labor. Thus, while raising wage rates, free trade reduces the market power of unions and reduces their ability to affect wage rates.

6. The implications of an FTAA for Latin America are considered by Corden (1995), who concludes that, with qualifications, Latin American countries "are highly likely to benefit from forming FTAs with the United States" (p. 30). Dornbusch (1995, 33) emphasizes that "free trade in the Western Hemisphere is in the common interest of all participants." For an emphasis on the qualifications, see Krueger (1995c).

7. For simplicity, we refer to Western Hemisphere countries south of the

The Hub-and-Spoke Issue

The issue of overlapping free trade arrangements arose at an early stage in the negotiations with Mexico: would there be two overlapping free trade agreements—with a new agreement between the United States and Mexico coming into force alongside the existing U.S.-Candian FTA—or would a single NAFTA be negotiated? In the event, there was a (more or less) single agreement, to which I will turn in just a moment. But before doing so, I note that this is not an issue that has been settled once and for all. On the contrary, there are straws in the wind that suggest that overlapping free trade arrangements may become a formidable issue for the future.

Just one month before the Miami summit, the participants in the Asia-Pacific Economic Cooperation (APEC) summit in Bogor, Indonesia, declared their vision of free trade within APEC by the year 2020, with the developed members' providing free access for their APEC partners' products by 2010. If the United States and other American members of APEC (Canada, Chile, and Mexico) proceed with both free trade visions—for the Americas and APEC—the result will be a stupendous hub-and-spoke system. The NAFTA countries plus Chile, which will be members of both FTAA and an APEC FTA, will be at the hub of a system including more than half the world's trade, with the Asian countries of APEC constituting one giant spoke and most Latin American countries another. The hub-and-spoke issue gains additional importance because of the continuing interest in a free trade agreement between North America and Europe. That proposal, which has been in the background for the past three decades, has recently begun to gain prominence with Canada's 1994 proposal for an FTA between NAFTA and Europe, with a somewhat similar proposal by a former U.S. Trade Representative in the *Wall Street Journal* (Yeutter and Murayama 1995) and by the current EU study of the idea. There have also been proposals for broader free trade between Europe and the Americas (Pena 1995), but as such proposals become comprehensive, the hub-and-spoke issue diminishes: more countries are included in core agreements and not left as spokes.

The Hub-and-Spoke Issue and the NAFTA Negotiations. When Mexico and the United States made preliminary contacts on the possibility of a free trade agreement in 1990, the initial assumption was that the negotiations would proceed on a bilateral basis. Canada, which al-

---

U.S. border as *Latin.* The term, as used here, should be taken to include Caribbean nations, some of which are not in fact "Latin."

ready had its own bilateral agreement with the United States, would not be included. Mexican trade with Canada was only a small fraction (4 percent) of its trade with the United States, so relatively little seemed at stake, not enough to justify the complications and possible delays that would be caused by a third party at the table. Furthermore, participation by Canada might raise a touchy question: would the recently ratified U.S.-Canadian free trade agreement be reopened as a part of the NAFTA negotiations, or would Mexico be simply presented with the U.S.-Canadian agreement on a take-it-or-leave-it basis?

Reopening the U.S.-Canadian agreement seemed unwise, given the tough Canadian election that had been fought over its ratification in 1988, an election in which opponents had played on fears of cheap Mexican imports flooding through the United States into the Canadian market, even in the absence of free trade agreements with Mexico. Mexico, however, could scarcely be expected to accept a take-it-or-leave-it offer; in particular, the Mexican Constitution placed restrictions on foreign participation in the petroleum industry, and this industry was just as sensitive for Mexicans as the cultural industry was for Canada—an industry for which Canada had negotiated an exemption in the U.S.-Canadian agreement. Finally, if Canada wanted to participate in free trade with the rest of North America, it was quite entitled to negotiate a bilateral free trade agreement with Mexico. Three bilaterals would, of course, be more complicated than a single one, but a single trilateral agreement would be more complicated to negotiate all at once at the beginning. At the time of the initial U.S.-Mexican contacts over a free trade arrangement, the issue seemed in the United States to be one of how to address complexity: would the complications be addressed up front, in a trilateral negotiation, or later, though a mop-up Mexican-Canadian bilateral and a possible follow-on negotiation to reduce inconsistencies among the three bilateral agreements? Canada was worried about the dangers of being left out, especially as a U.S.-Mexican agreement was expected to be just the forerunner of a series of agreements with Latin American countries. In particular, Canada was concerned about the disadvantages of being just one of the spokes in a series of U.S. bilateral free trade agreements.

Because of these concerns, Canada became a full participant at the table. The "no modification, take-it-or-leave-it" dilemma was finessed. In most respects there is one trilateral agreement, which can be looked on as an extension of the U.S.-Canadian FTA. But in some other respects there are three coherent but partly separate agreements. Canada, for example, retained its exemption for cultural industries; there is no similar exception for Mexico. For its part, Mexico retained protection in the petroleum industry, which satisfied its constitutional requirements; but, as a result, Mexican commitments in this industry are very different from the arrangements between the United States and Canada. In general, the changes in the U.S.-Canadian agreement were relatively minor; the U.S.-Canadian FTA was reopened, but only a crack, and not enough to cause a major controversy in Canada. One change was in the automobile industry, where the North American content required to meet the rule of origin was increased from 50 percent to 62.5 percent, an increase that Canada resisted; the 62.5 percent was a compromise from the 65 percent suggested by the United States. Although Canada did not like the increase in the percentage, it did like the change in the way of calculating content to avoid a repeat of the Honda case,[8] where the U.S. Treasury had ruled that Canadian-built Hondas had not met the origin requirement under the U.S.-Canadian FTA. But the basic rules covering U.S.-Canadian automotive trade, which traced back to the U.S.-Canadian Auto Pact of 1965 and were grandfathered in the U.S.-Canadian FTA, remained essentially unchanged. Thus, the rules covering U.S.-Canadian and U.S.-Mexican automotive trade will remain somewhat different, even after the transition period. In agriculture, there were separate bilateral agreements, in effect, a set of three bilaterals stapled together in a single document. In spite of such untidiness, Canadians got their primary wish: inclusion in the negotiations and a simultaneous coming into force of the whole trilateral agreement.

Furthermore, the die had been cast for future negotiations. Rather than a bilateral with Chile, the United States will participate in an expansion of NAFTA to include Chile. This is a fortunate outcome, because of the problems raised by a hub-and-spoke system.[9]

Problems Raised by a Hub and Spokes. Suppose, to use a simple hypothetical illustration, that the United States and Mexico had engaged in a bilateral negotiation rather than including Canada. As a result, the United States would have been at the hub of two overlapping free trade areas: the existing U.S.-Canadian FTA and the new U.S.-Mexican agreement. This would have created a number of inefficiencies and disadvantages for Canada and Mexico, the two "spokes" of the system:

---

8. The change in the way of calculating content means that the change in the requirement in the automotive industry is generally less than implied by the increase from 50 percent to 62.5 percent, but the effects differ among various automotive products.

9. Early hub-and-spoke literature includes Ronald J. Wonnacott (1975a, where the term *two-sided triangle* was used, 1982, 1990), Park and Yoo (1989, who write of a system of a star and its points), and Lipsey (1990).

• Exports of the hub country (the United States) would have had a preference in the markets of the spoke countries; that is, the exports of spoke countries to each other would have faced discrimination in competing with duty-free exports from the hub. Similarly, only firms in the hub country would have had access to duty-free imported inputs from each spoke.

• Locations in the United States, with their duty-free access to both Canada and Mexico, would have had an advantage in attracting plants. Canadian locations would have been at a disadvantage, since they would have had duty-free access only to the United States and not to Mexico, and Mexican locations would have had a similar disadvantage.

• Some trade between Mexico and Canada would have been redirected through the United States, in cases where enough U.S. value could be added to meet the rule of origin and thus qualify for duty-free passage. In some cases, Canadian and Mexican parts would have been assembled in the United States to take advantage of the duty-free passage to both contiguous countries.

In part, the disadvantages to each spoke in a hub-and-spoke system are similar to the disadvantages of any country left out of a free-trade agreement. A bilateral U.S.-Mexican FTA, for example, would have given U.S. exports a preference in the Mexican market over Canadian exports; but it would also have given U.S. exports a preference over exports from any other outside location, such as Europe or East Asia. The disadvantage to Canadian and Mexican exports would, however, have been even greater because, with free access to both spoke markets, U.S. locations would have had an advantage in attracting new plants. This would have been a special concern to Canada; locations on the two sides of the border are engaged in strong competition because of the similarity of the two economies and because most of the Canadian population lives close to the border.

It might seem that Canada and Mexico would have been in a position to overcome these disadvantages in a straightforward and obvious way, by negotiating a bilateral agreement between them, thus completing the third side of the triangle. Rather than a hub country with two spokes, there would then have been three countries joined by three bilateral agreements. While such a third bilateral would have formally put the countries in similar positions, however, it would not have been an adequate solution for the two smaller countries, because of the advantage the larger country has in meeting the rules of origin.

Rules of Origin

Because an FTA allows each member to set its own tariff on outside countries, it requires rules of origin. Otherwise, there would be an incentive for trade deflection—that is, imports would come into the FTA through the low-tariff country and be transshipped duty-free into the high-tariff country. Rules of origin (ROOs), which must be met to qualify for duty-free passage between members of an FTA, are usually specified in several ways: a certain percentage of the value added must originate within the members of the FTA (for example, the 62.5 percent requirement for autos in the NAFTA), or a product must include a specific component produced within the FTA (for example, in the U.S.-Canadian agreement, this was the motherboard for personal computers),[10] or a good imported from an outside country must be transformed enough to cause it to move to another tariff classification.[11] (Sometimes—as in the case of textiles in NAFTA—the product must be transformed through several tariff classifications.)

While rules of origin must be included in an FTA in which member countries have significantly different tariffs against outsiders, they raise several difficulties. One is the cost of extra bookkeeping to meet the sometimes complicated rules[12]—a cost that has been rising as production becomes more integrated internationally (for example, in automobiles and parts of the electronics industry). This cost is sufficiently high that some North American firms have decided that they would rather skip the bookkeeping and instead pay the MFN tariff on their exports to NAFTA partner countries. In such cases, the advantages of the FTA are obviously lost. A second problem is the disagreement that may arise between FTA members as to whether the value-added requirements have been met; the dispute over Canadian-built Hondas under the U.S.-Canadian FTA was a notable example. A third issue is that rules of origin may be changed to make them more demanding

---

10. One of the controversial issues in the NAFTA negotiations was whether there would be a new origin requirement for PCs, that the flat panel display be produced in North America. (The motherboard had declined in importance, and the display increased, since the earlier U.S.-Canadian FTA.) In the event, there was no such specific requirement for the flat panel display, in part because of opposition by the computer manufacturers. (An antidumping duty on flat panel displays had already driven some computer production offshore, to Ireland and elsewhere.)

11. Palmeter (1995, 205–6) concludes that the change in tariff heading is probably the best ROO for an FTA, although it is particularly susceptible to manipulation by rent-seekers.

12. Herin (1986) estimated the bookkeeping costs associated with meeting rules of origin in the European Free Trade Association were in the range of 3–5 percent of prices. The bookkeeping costs of rules of origin, and their possible abuse for protective purposes, are major reasons why Krueger (1995a, b) concludes that FTAs are less likely to improve efficiency than are CUs.

and thus make it more difficult for producers to meet them, while at the same time increasing the level of protection.

Smaller countries in an FTA also see another disadvantage: although value added in all member countries counts, rules of origin give businesses an incentive to locate in the largest market. Most obviously, if bookkeeping costs are sufficiently high to consider paying the MFN tariff instead, there is an advantage in exporting from the large to the small economy: the market on which MFN tariffs will be paid is smaller than if exports go the opposite way.

Another complication from the rules of origin—the complication most relevant for the present discussion—has to do with the hub-and-spoke problem. Suppose, to return to the earlier example, that, instead of NAFTA, the United States had entered a bilateral FTA with Mexico. If Canada and Mexico had tried to deal with the spoke problem by negotiating their own bilateral FTA, they would still have faced a disadvantage. Parts exports from Canada to Mexico, for example, which were then included in Mexican-built cars destined for the United States, would not have counted as content under the bilateral U.S.-Mexican FTA. This would have discouraged parts exports from Canada to Mexico and car exports from Mexico to the United States. Again, this complication raises greater problems for the smaller than for the larger country, because a larger percentage of value added generally originates in the larger country.

This complication could be solved in two ways. The first would be a follow-up negotiation by the three countries to transform the three bilaterals into a single NAFTA; the NAFTA result would eventually be achieved, but in a piecemeal, drawn-out way with additional adjustment costs. Second, where there are overlapping FTAs, the hub may be prepared to count content *regardless of which spoke is its country of origin* (that is, to count content even where it has been shipped from one spoke to another). The latter has been done by the European Union in its FTAs with several Central European countries.

With a simple, clean customs union with its common external tariff, there is no need for rules of origin, just as there is no need for such rules in trade among the states of a single country. (Some rules of origin existed within the European Community, however, in cases where individual countries maintained quotas or other nontariff barriers on imports from outside the EC, which meant that the EC did not have common external barriers in all respects.)

Free Trade Agreements Compared with Customs Union

Thus far, this chapter has looked at several areas where a customs union is superior to an FTA. As just noted, rules of origin, with their accounting and administrative costs, are unnecessary in a CU. Furthermore, the hub-and-spoke problem does not arise in a standard CU, since the common external tariff means that members cannot go off on their own, signing bilaterals with outside nations. To establish our major conclusion—in favor of a modified FTA rather than a CU for the Americas—it is essential to point out some of the disadvantages of a CU. We look at two: the political implications of a CU and the greater ease of reducing tariffs in an FTA.

Political Implications of Integrated Decision Making. Because FTA members maintain their own individual tariffs on outside countries while CU members commit themselves to a common external tariff, a CU requires a greater degree of cooperation and collective decision making. This is especially so if a CU develops into a common market, with internal factor mobility and mutual recognition of each other's safety, health, and other product standards. And it is even more so if the members decide to work toward a common currency.

This closer cooperation may sometimes be seen as a plus, quite apart from the possible economic gains; indeed, one of the objectives in the establishment of the European Community (now the European Union) was to promote joint decision making and reduce the nationalisms that have been so destructive historically.

In other circumstances, however, it may be a disadvantage. The joint decision making implied by a customs union is precisely why this option was unattractive in North America. For Canada and later Mexico, the clear political disadvantage of a CU was that, realistically, the common external tariff would be determined in Washington; the United States obviously has by far the largest economy. South American countries are likely to have the same reservations. At the same time, it is unlikely that the United States would be willing to enter a CU if it thereby had to commit itself not to change any of its tariffs unless it first got agreement from other countries in the hemisphere.

FTAs, Easier Reductions in Barriers. An FTA has the advantage that tariffs on outsiders may be more easily reduced than with a CU. Because nations in an FTA are not committed to a common external tariff, they have the ability—as well as an incentive—to cut tariffs on parts and other inputs to improve their competitive positions within the FTA. This is particularly the case where their tariffs on inputs are greater than those of the other members of the FTA and the domestic industry can argue that tariffs on inputs must be cut to eliminate its competitive disadvantage. At the beginning of 1994, for example, Canada cut its MFN tariffs on many parts for automotive engines and transmissions from 9.2 percent to either 2.5 percent or zero. Other unilateral cuts are now under consideration.

A nation in an FTA also has an incentive to cut tariffs in situations where its consumers are paying high prices for goods imported from its FTA partners—that is, *precisely in those products where trade diversion is taking place.* The consumers who are hurt are in the importing country and in a position to complain to their government, which sets the tariff; the producers who benefit are in one of the other FTA countries. In the political struggle between consumer and producer over tariffs, the producer is generally successful (unless exporting producers can be brought to bear in the decision-making process). If the contest is between the interests of the domestic consumer and producer in one of the other FTA countries, however, the outcome may well swing the other way, toward consumers with their interest in lower trade barriers. In contrast, in a CU with its collective decision making on the common external tariff, there is greater opportunity for producer interests to triumph and establish a coalition to set a high tariff or block a tariff reduction.

To make the general point in a different way: Europe's Common Agricultural Policy would not have occurred if there had been an FTA rather than a CU. For example, if Britain had been joining an FTA rather than a CU, it would undoubtedly have continued to import many of its agricultural imports from cheap overseas sources.

Because there is a greater tendency for trade barriers to be stuck at a high level in a CU than in an FTA, a CU is more likely to create a situation in which one of the member countries feels that it is being exploited by serving as a captive market for the high-cost protected products made in a partner country.

The common external tariff can therefore put strains on a CU— just as an ordinary national tariff can create regional strains within a nation-state. There are numerous examples. In the nineteenth century, early talk of nullification of federal law in the U.S. South was inspired by the tariff: the South viewed itself as the captive market for high-priced, protected Northern manufactures. In contrast, the North did not serve as a captive market for the South to the same extent: disproportionate amounts of Southern products (cotton, tobacco) were sold on world markets. A similar problem existed in Canada, where the Western Provinces felt exploited by having to buy high-priced manufactures from Ontario and Quebec,[13] while they—like the nineteenth

---

13. For example, Shearer, Young, and Munro (1971, 203) concluded that:

> Western Canada—and specifically British Columbia—suffers from being in a customs union with the rest of the country; the central

century American South—sold their wheat and other resource-based products on world markets. Thus, while Canada's free trade with the United States weakened Canadian nationalism in some respects, it also reduced this source of east-west strain on Canadian unity.

Similar strains have occurred in customs unions: for example, in 1992 Ecuador refused to accept the common external tariff proposed by the other members of the Andean Pact because it wanted to continue to import from cheap outside sources rather than rely on high-cost producers in other member nations.[14] In general, such strains have contributed to the lack of success of inward-looking, protectionist CUs in the third world. In the MERCOSUR customs union, it will be interesting to see if Argentina comes to see itself as an exploited market for high-priced Brazilian manufactures. (The risks of such a perception have, however, been reduced because MERCOSUR is not adopting a common external tariff on all goods but allows nationally set tariffs on capital goods and high-tech items. Thus, MERCOSUR has adopted an intermediate system between a CU and an FTA, somewhat similar to that recommended in this chapter.)

An FTA has the advantage that "exploited countries" can escape their difficulty very simply, by cutting their MFN tariffs on the products they import at high cost from their partners.

An Intermediate System? Thus, an FTA has a major advantage, from a free trade viewpoint, in providing incentives and the opportunity for individual members to cut some of their tariffs and other trade barriers. In contrast, a CU has a major advantage in avoiding rules of origin.[15]

How these two advantages compare depends importantly on the height of tariffs. The lower tariff rates are already, the less is to be gained by the remaining tariff cuts that can be made by individual FTA

---

provinces [Ontario and Quebec] suffer from not being in a customs union with the rest of the world.

Interestingly, Quebec was strongly in favor of the free trade agreement with the United States, while Ontario was negative.

14. For details on the Andean Pact and other American regional arrangements, see Hufbauer and Schott (1994, appendix C, especially p. 235).

15. This chapter puts forward a case for an intermediate system, arguing that FTAs and CUs each have advantages, and that many of the advantages of each can be combined in a hybrid system. For the case that a CU is preferable to an FTA, see Krueger (1995a, 1995b) and Panagariya and Findlay (1994). For the case in which an FTA gives an incentive for each country to reduce its external tariffs, see Sinclair and Vines (1994). For a recent survey, see Frankel (1995).

members. At the same time, the bookkeeping costs of rules of origin remain regardless of the height of tariffs; indeed, they become higher as tariffs fall and production becomes more integrated internationally. (Nevertheless, as noted above, if tariffs are low enough, a company may simply skip the content bookkeeping and pay the MFN tariff of its partner instead.)

Thus, the lower tariffs are, the stronger the case is for a CU compared to an FTA. Accordingly, as tariffs have been negotiated down in recent decades, the case for a CU has strengthened compared with that for an FTA. It has also strengthened as free trade arrangements have proliferated in the Americas, creating not just hubs and spokes but an even more confusing, tangled web of agreements that Jules Katz has referred to as "spaghetti." Because a CU, with its common external tariff, limits the freedom of individual members to enter into side agreements with outside nations, the question therefore arises, Should we be thinking of a CU of the Americas rather than an FTAA? We might be tempted to answer yes, but to do so we would have to solve the fundamental difficulty already noted: the dominance of the United States and the unwillingness of other countries of the Americas simply to sign on to a tariff made in Washington, on the one hand, and the reluctance of the United States to share its decision making on commercial policies, on the other. Perhaps, then, the above question should be modified: Is there scope for a further development of an intermediate arrangement between a pure FTA and a CU? That is, what is to be said for a system with a common external tariff in some products, which will then be exempt from rules of origin, while FTA arrangements, with their rules of origin, are retained in other industries? This question has already arisen in the NAFTA agreement on computers, where there will be a "matching external tariff"—in effect, a common external tariff—which will move to zero and eliminate the rule of origin.

There are several major intermediate systems from which a choice might be made.

- The most obvious would be to have CU rules (a common external tariff and no rules of origin) for some products on which agreement could be reached, with FTA rules applying to all other products.
- A second option would be a standard free trade agreement with one important modification: rules of origin would be eliminated for products on which all members adopted a tariff no higher than some low cutoff rate, for example, 2 percent or 3 percent. With tariffs so low, the problem of transshipment (trade deflection), which rules of origin (ROOs) are intended to solve, would have little importance; the rules

of origin would not be missed. In contrast to option 1, members would retain the right to change all their external tariffs (with increases being subject to GATT bindings) without the agreement of their partners, thus reducing concerns about "exploitation" or about the tariff being "set in Washington." There would presumably have to be an agreement that, if a country raised its external tariff above the cutoff rate, it would not be able to restore the rule of origin; otherwise, each member would have the power to reintroduce a rule of origin in specific industries (depending on its GATT bindings), and member countries could not count on industries remaining "ROOless." Because members could not unilaterally reinstate rules of origin on the agreed-upon products, no member would be likely to raise its tariff unilaterally on these products substantially, since it would be exposed to trade deflection through the other members. Thus, the liberalizing tendency of an FTA would be maintained. New members would undertake not to impose rules of origin on these products.

• A third option would extend the set of "ROOless" industries further. Rules of origin would not be applied by any member country to products where the *range* between the highest and the lowest external tariffs was no greater than some low cutoff rate, say, 2 percent. As in the previous case, there would presumably have to be an agreement that, if a country raised its external tariff to move it outside the range, that country would not be able to restore the rule of origin. In this case, however, there would also be a second question: if a country unilaterally cuts its external tariff to put it below the lower limit of the range, would its FTA partners have the right to reintroduce a ROO? On that, I have no recommendation; let me leave it as a loose end. One further complication would also arise in this third option: tariff revenues under this provision might be significant, in which case the question of the sharing of these revenues would arise, as it does in a customs union.

• A fourth option would be to have no rule of origin for a specific product in the country with the lowest tariff on that product,[16] or in all member countries with tariffs within some small range (say, 2 percent) of the lowest tariff on that product.

---

16. I am indebted to Gary Hufbauer, who pointed out this option in his comments on a previous draft of this chapter at the conference "Capital Flows and Regionalism," sponsored by the Center for International Economics, University of Maryland, and the American Enterprise Institute, June 13, 1995. The idea that a ROO is unnecessary for the low-tariff country may also be found in R. J. Wonnacott, (1975b, 82 fn8).

These options are not mutually exclusive; a combination might be adopted. I would recommend the adoption of the first three: there would be no rules of origin for three sets of products, namely those where (1) a common external tariff was agreed upon; or (2) all members adopted a low tariff (less than 2 percent or 3 percent); or (3) the external tariffs of members fell in a narrow range of, say, 2 percent.[17]

The fourth option is also worth study, although I have some hesitation to recommend it. One possible problem is that, unlike the situation with the first three options, ROOs would be asymmetrically eliminated by the country or countries with the lowest tariff on the specific product, but not the countries with the high tariffs. Countries might then be reluctant to reduce their tariffs.

Another problem with the fourth option, and to some extent with all the options, is that, in the absence of an across-the-board CET, most-favored nation tariffs may differ among member countries not only on final products but also on inputs. Trade deflection can occur both when a final product comes in through a low-tariff member country and then is transshipped to a higher-tariff member country, and when parts are imported into the member with low tariffs on parts and are then assembled into a final product for export to partner countries even where the assembly process may be high cost. Rules of origin can limit this type of deflection. Thus, for any of the above ways of avoiding ROOs, tariffs on parts and other inputs might have to be considered, too. The second option above, for example, could be elaborated to require not only tariffs of 2 to 3 percent or less on the final product but also no more than 2 or 3 percent on inputs, on average. That might not be much of a problem—products with low final tariffs also tend to have low tariffs on inputs—but it does illustrate how negotiations over the above options might become complicated. The ultimate objective of the options should not be lost, however. Even though they can make the negotiating process more complex, they are a way of simplifying business activity, specifically by eliminating the administrative and bookkeeping for ROOs for the products falling under the above options.

---

17. The question might be raised whether options 1 and 2 are not simply subsets of option 3. The answer is, not quite. In option 1, tariffs are clearly within 2 percent; but the idea of having some products with a CET is worth maintaining separately, since a CET has special implications for the rules of accession, as explained below. Option 2 is not necessarily a subset of option 3, because the range might be set somewhat broader (as suggested by the 3 percent in the example) in cases where the lower boundary is a tariff of zero. A broader band might be acceptable, since the revenue-sharing complications become unimportant when tariffs are very low.

Thus, there may be a trade-off between complexity in negotiations and complexities faced by businesses in the resulting FTA.

Finally, nontariff barriers may complicate the elimination of ROOs. That complication, however, can also arise in a customs union, such as the European Union, where ROOs have not been eliminated. Thus, this is a general complication of regional arrangements, not one specific to the type of intermediate or hybrid system being considered here. To reiterate the main objective of an intermediate system: by getting rid of rules of origin for a significant fraction of products, a hybrid FTA could gain many of the advantages of a CU without requiring a commitment to an across-the-board CET.

In addition to avoiding ROOs, having at least some products in the first category, with a CET, offers a further advantage. *Provided there were at least some CETs set above zero,* no individual member or small group of members would be able to negotiate independent free trade agreements with outside countries, since the original agreement would not allow them to undercut the agreed-upon CET. In other words, the arrangements on the entry of new members would be the same as with a CU. The idea would be to establish the mind set of a CU, in which individual union partners do not even think about signing independent agreements with outsiders.

An agreement to a (nonzero) CET in at least some products would not only prevent any member from becoming a hub by signing side deals with outsiders but also prevent its partners from so doing, and thus assure the member that it would not itself become a spoke. But it would not flatly prevent a hub-and-spoke system from developing, with the original FTA as a whole at the hub of a system. In this case, the original FTA would follow the rules of a customs union, such as the European Union, in negotiating with outside countries. But a customs union can negotiate FTAs with outside countries, becoming the hub of a hub-and-spoke system, as the European Union has in fact done with a number of countries in Central Europe (Baldwin 1994; Enders and Wonnacott 1995). (As noted earlier, the hub-and-spoke problem has been reduced by the EU's cumulative rule of origin that counts content from any of the countries with agreements with the EU.)

Rules of Accession

It might seem that the first option, with its commitment to common action for any new arrangements with outside countries, is not very important for NAFTA as it considers new members from South America. After all, NAFTA *already* has a clause that requires unanimous agreement before new members are admitted. But this accession clause is not so strong as it seems. Suppose, to use a counterfactual example, that Canada did not want Chile to be admitted to NAFTA. The United States could initiate a bilateral negotiation with Chile (or a trilateral with Chile and Mexico). Canada could scarcely stay out, since its absence would leave it as a spoke, with the attendant disadvantages. In other words, under current NAFTA rules, two closely interrelated problems (or, conceivably, advantages?) arise. First, members of NAFTA are not precluded from individually entering agreements with outside nations, thus making their current NAFTA partners into spokes of the new arrangements. And second, each of the NAFTA members, and particularly the United States, has the power to pressure its partners to accept a new member: it can declare its intention to negotiate an independent agreement if its partners object to the proposed new member. In contrast, with a CET in some products, customs union rules for entering free-trade negotiations with outsiders would prevail; such negotiations would require agreement among existing members. As the FTA expands, the unanimity rule might be relaxed. Once MERCOSUR is admitted, for example, it might as a group have a veto over further admissions, without each of the two small countries (Paraguay and Uruguay) having a veto.

Where Do We Go from Here?

The above proposals are aimed at two objectives: reducing the number of industries in which rules of origin need to be enforced and providing some discipline in the process, to prevent the proliferation of hubs and spokes or even more complex arrangements (Jules Katz's "spaghetti"). Three major complications arise: the existing commitment to an APEC free trade agreement; the possibility of an FTA with Europe; and existing arrangements that complicate a clean outcome, for example, the U.S.-Israel FTA and U.S. arrangements with the countries of the Caribbean Basin.

FTAA and APEC. To propose rules to prevent the development of hubs and spokes might seem fanciful, when the United States (and others) are on record in favor of an APEC free trade agreement (APEC 1994). How can this major complication be dealt with?

One possibility is to temporize for a year or two. Chile is a relatively uncomplicated case, and decisions on the design of an FTAA might reasonably be left somewhat vague for the moment. But during the negotiations with MERCOSUR, we should be making these decisions.

Temporization may be enough to deal with the APEC issue. I

frankly doubt that an APEC FTA will get beyond the vision stage.[18] In particular, I do not envy the American official who would have to march up to Capitol Hill and explain why the United States should have free trade with China (or Japan, for that matter) and why, in particular, the United States should grant *unilateral* free trade to China for a ten-year period (2010–2020). If enthusiasm for an APEC FTA wanes, the question of a huge Pacific hub and spoke would become moot.

If, as seems improbable, strong moves toward an APEC FTA occur, then the hub-and-spoke problem could be handled by giving all members of an FTAA the option of joining the APEC FTA. Alternatively, the nations of the FTAA could negotiate as a group with the Asian members of APEC.

My doubts regarding an APEC FTA do not reflect skepticism toward APEC as such. Tariffs are no longer the center of international economic policies; there are many other important areas of cooperation. I certainly support the APEC process, dealing with trade, investment, communications, and intellectual property relations with the very important countries of East Asia. I also support cooperative arrangements, such as those for simplified and faster customs clearance. The process of cooperation feeds on itself; it helps political leaders to think in terms of closer economic relations. On the specific question of tariffs, I think that there is scope for regional negotiations, especially if they proceed on an MFN basis.[19] But I have doubts about the feasibility of an APEC FTA as put forward at Bogor.

FTAA and Europe. If we were to proceed with both an APEC FTA and a transatlantic FTA, we would be quickly drawn far beyond hub-and-spoke issues to even more basic questions. Because such arrangements would cover the great preponderance of the world's trade, we would have to consider how the various FTAs might be folded into one big agreement—assuming that this question had not already been faced before the negotiation of the large FTAs. And who then would be left out? Would it make sense to have a huge FTA excluding much of the developing world? Would it not make sense to fold such negotiations into a new multilateral WTO negotiation, perhaps reverting to conditional MFN arrangements for all those who wished to join agreements on the more controversial subjects (such as was done for the subsidies

---

18. For other skeptical views regarding an APEC FTA, see Panagariya (1994).

19. On nondiscriminatory liberalization, see Anderson (1991); Drysdale and Garnaut (1989, 1993); Petri (1992); P. Wonnacott (1995); and the World Bank (1993).

code in the Tokyo Round)? This sort of question may have led to the puzzling concept of "open regionalism" in APEC. Presumably, the idea is to strengthen internal ties without withdrawing into a block, either by admitting new members freely or extending internal commitments to other countries on an MFN basis. Some proponents of an APEC FTA see it as a way of creating a momentum that will encourage the European Union to respond with broad initiatives of its own.

At any rate, any European arrangement with NAFTA or an expanded FTAA seems to be quite far down on the U.S. list of options. News reports in June 1995 that Secretary of State Warren Christopher had pledged to study free trade with Europe were apparently incomplete and did not accurately reflect the major thrust of his remarks. The United States will welcome broad talks aimed at deepening and strengthening security, economic, and political relations in the twenty-first century. Economic topics would include such subjects as investment rules, telecommunications and other information and technology markets, product standards, and financial services. As I understand it, the report in the *Financial Times* (White and Jonquieres 1995) was accurate: Mr. Christopher "appeared cautious about recent European suggestions that the two sides should seek to negotiate a transatlantic free trade agreement."

Israel and the Caribbean. Free trade agreements covering APEC or joining the EU with America would fundamentally change the world trading system. In contrast, the U.S.-Israel free trade agreement and the U.S. Caribbean Basin Initiative (CBI) are sufficiently narrow in their effects as to be treated as special cases. For Israel, the CETs adopted by an FTAA might include a grandfathered exception: the United States could keep its free trade agreement with Israel.

The CBI might also be grandfathered. But one-way preferences reduce the degree of openness of countries; they are based on Prebisch's old idea that, in the absence of one-way preferences, gains from trade go predominantly to the richer countries—a proposition that is just as questionable as Ross Perot's opposite fear of a "giant sucking sound." Rather than having a grandfathering of the CBI, the Caribbean nations should be included in an FTAA. There would, however, have to be a grandfathering of special relationships that some Caribbean countries already have with Europe.

The trouble with grandfathering is that it introduces risk into the policy of temporizing suggested above. As we allow things to slide, new arrangements may develop, calling for additional grandfathering of exceptions to the structure of an FTAA. For the United States, and indeed for the other NAFTA countries and other potential FTAA members as well, a choice lies before us: Do we want to "let anything go," in order to keep open the door for an APEC FTA or an FTA with Europe? Or do we want to tighten up the rules, perhaps along the lines noted above, in order to prevent a proliferation of inconsistent and overlapping free trade associations?

I have already suggested an answer. Before we get very far into discussions with MERCOSUR, we should consider institutional arrangements of an FTAA in detail. In particular, we should decide whether we want to develop a hybrid FTA.

Conclusions

In summary, there are both advantages and disadvantages in free trade associations compared with customs unions. On the one hand, an FTA permits, and can encourage, individual nations to reduce their external tariffs, particularly in cases where trade diversion is occurring. On the other hand, a CU generally avoids rules of origin, which can be administratively expensive and protective in their effects. FTAs and CUs differ also in two other ways: a CU requires a greater degree of political coordination or integration to develop its common external tariff, and a CU's CET acts to constrain individual members from negotiating agreements with outside countries. That is, it constrains the development of hub-and-spoke systems. The greater coordination may in some circumstances be an advantage and, in others, a disadvantage.

This chapter recommends an intermediate system for a Free Trade Association of the Americas. There would be a common external tariff on some products, with member nations maintaining their own national tariffs on outside countries for other products. There would be no rules of origin for three sets of products: those where a common external tariff was agreed upon; those where all members adopted a low tariff (less than 2 percent or 3 percent); or those where the external tariffs of members fell in a narrow range of, say, 2 percent.

This intermediate system would have several advantages. It would provide greater national independence than a CU; like a CU, it would act as a constraint on the development of hub-and-spoke systems; and it would remove onerous rules of origin on some products.

References

Anderson, Kym. "Is an Asia-Pacific Bloc Next?" *Journal of World Trade,* vol. 25–4, 1991, pp. 27–40.
APEC. "APEC Economic Leaders' Declaration of Common Resolve." Bogor, Indonesia, Nov. 15, 1994.

Baldwin, Richard. *Towards an Integrated Europe*. London: Centre for Economic Policy Research, 1994.

Bergsten, C. Fred, and Marcus Noland, eds. *Pacific Dynamism and the International Economic System*. Washington, D.C.: Institute for International Economics, 1993.

Caves, Richard, Michael E. Porter, and A. Michael Spence. *Competition in the Open Economy*. Cambridge, Mass.: Harvard University Press, 1980.

Caves, Richard, Michael E. Porter, A. Michael Spence, John P. Scott, and Andre Lemelin. *Studies in Canadian Industrial Organization*. Ottawa: Royal Commission on Corporate Concentration, 1977.

Colombo, John R. *Colombo's Canadian Quotations*. Edmonton: Hurtig Publishers, 1974.

Corden, W. Max. "A Western Hemisphere Free-Trade Area: Implications for Latin America." In IDB and ECLAC, *Trade Liberalization in the Western Hemisphere*. Washington, D.C.: ECLAC, 1995.

Dornbusch, Rudiger. "North-South Trade Relations in the Americas: The Case for Free Trade." In IDB and ECLAC, *Trade Liberalization in the Western Hemisphere*. Washington, D.C.: ECLAC, 1995.

Drysdale, Peter, and Ross Garnaut. "A Pacific Free-Trade Area?" In Jeffrey J. Schott, ed., *Free Trade Areas and U.S. Trade Policy*. Washington, D.C.: Institute for International Economics, 1989.

———. "The Pacific: An Application of the General Theory of Economic Integration." In Fred C. Bergsten and Marcus Noland, eds., *Dynamism and the International Economic System*. Washington, D.C.: Institute for International Economics, 1993.

Eastman, Harry C., and Stefan Stykolt. *The Tariff and Competition in Canada*. Toronto: Macmillan, 1967.

Enders, Alice, and Ronald J. Wonnacott. "Hub-and-Spoke and Other Patterns in East-West European Trade Liberalization." London, Canada: University of Western Ontario, Centre for the Study of International Economic Relations. Working Paper, 1995.

English, H. Edward. *Industrial Structure in Canada's International Competitive Position*. Montreal: Private Planning Association of Canada, 1964.

Frankel, Jeffrey A. "Does Regionalism Undermine Multilateral Trade Liberalization or Support It?" Washington, D.C.: Institute for International Economics, 1995.

Granatstein, J. L. "Free Trade between Canada and the United States: The Issue That Will Not Go Away." In Denis Stairs and Gilbert R. Winham, eds., *The Politics of Canada's Economic Relationship with the United States*. Toronto: University of Toronto Press in cooperation with the Royal Commission on the Economic Union and Development Prospects for Canada, 1955.

Harris, Richard G., with David Cox. *Trade, Industrial Policy and Canadian Manufacturing*. Toronto: Ontario Economic Council, 1984.

Herin, Jan. "Rules of Origin and Differences between Tariff Levels in EFTA and in the EC." Geneva: EFTA Occasional Paper 13, February 1986.

Hufbauer, Gary C., and Jeffrey J. Schott. *Western Hemisphere Economic Integration*. Washington, D.C.: Institute for International Economics, 1994.

Inter-American Development Bank (IDB) and Economic Commission for Latin America and the Caribbean (ECLAC). *Trade Liberalization in the Western Hemisphere*. Washington, D.C.: ECLAC, 1995.

Krueger, Anne O. "Trade-Creating and Trade-Busting Aspects of NAFTA." Paper prepared for American Economic Association Meetings. Stanford University, January 1995a.

———. "Free Trade Agreements vs. Customs Unions." NBER Working Paper 5084, April 1995b.

———. "Conditions for Maximizing the Gains from a WHFTA." In IDB and ECLAC, *Trade Liberalization in the Western Hemisphere*. Washington, D.C.: ECLAC, 1995c.

Lipsey, Richard G. "Canada and the U.S.-Mexico Free Trade Dance: Wallflower or Partner?" Toronto: C. D. Howe Institute, 1990, Commentary 20.

Okuizume, K, K. E. Calder, and G. W. Gong, eds. *The U.S.-Japan Economic Relationship in East and Southeast Asia*. Washington, D.C.: Center for Strategic and International Studies, 1992.

Palmeter, N. David. "Rules of Origin in a Western Hemisphere Free Trade Agreement." In IDB and ECLAC, *Trade Liberalization in the Western Hemisphere*. Washington, D.C.: ECLAC, 1995.

Panagariya, Arvind. "East Asia and the New Regionalism." *The World Economy*, vol. 17, November 1994, pp. 817–40.

Panagariya, Arvind, and Ronald Findlay. "A Political Economy Analysis of Free Trade Areas and Customs Unions." College Park: University of Maryland, Center for International Economics, 1994.

Park, Yung C., and Jung Ho Yoo. "More Free Trade Areas: A Korean Perspective." In Jeffrey J. Schott, ed., *Free Trade Areas and U.S. Trade Policy*. Washington D.C.: Institute for International Economics, 1989.

Pastor, Robert A. "The North American Free Trade Agreement: Hemispheric and Geopolitical Implications." In IDB and ECLAC, *Trade Liberalization in the Western Hemisphere*. Washington, D.C.: ECLAC, 1995.

Pena, Felix. "Hemispheric Free Trade: NAFTA vs. MERCOSUR." *The Washington Quarterly*, vol. 18, Summer 1995, pp. 113–22.

Petri, Peter. "One Bloc, Two Blocs, or None? Political-Economic Factors in Pacific Trade Policy." In K. Okuizume, K. E. Calder, and G. W.

Gong, eds., *The U.S.-Japan Economic Relationship in East and Southeast Asia*. Washington, D.C.: Center for Strategic and International Studies, 1992.

Royal Commission on the Economic Union and Development Prospects for Canada (the Macdonald Commission). *Report*, vol. 1. Ottawa, 1985.

Schott, Jeffrey J., ed. *Free Trade Areas and U.S. Trade Policy*. Washington, D.C.: Institute for International Economics, 1989.

Shearer, R. A., J. H. Young, and G. R. Munro. *Trade Liberalization and a Regional Economy: Studies of the Impact of Free Trade on British Columbia*. Toronto: University of Toronto Press for the Private Planning Association of Canada, 1971.

Sinclair, Peter, and David Vines. "Do Fewer, Larger Trade Blocs Imply Greater Protection?" University of Birmingham and Oxford University, June 1994.

Spence, A. M. "Efficiency, Scale, and Trade in Canadian and United States Manufacturing Industries." In Richard Caves, Michael E. Porter, A. Michael Spence, John P. Scott, and Andre Lemelin, *Studies in Canadian Industrial Organization*. Ottawa: Royal Commission on Corporate Concentration, 1977.

———. "Efficiency, Scale, and Trade in Canadian and U.S. Manufacturing Industries." In Richard Caves, Michael E. Porter, and A. Michael Spence, *Competition in the Open Economy*. Cambridge, Mass.: Harvard University Press, 1980.

Stairs, Denis, and Gilbert R. Winham, eds. *The Politics of Canada's Economic Relationship with the United States*. Toronto: University of Toronto Press in cooperation with the Royal Commission on the Economic Union and Development Prospects for Canada, 1985.

Waite, Peter. *Canada 1874–1896: Arduous Destiny*. Toronto: McClelland and Stewart, 1971.

Weintraub, Sidney. "Resurgence and Uncertainty in Argentina, Brazil, and Chile." New York: Conference Board, Global Business White Papers, no. 16, April 1995.

White, David, and Guy de Jonquieres. "U.S. Calls for Talks to Improve Links with Europe." *Financial Times*, June 3, 1995.

Wonnacott, Paul. *The United States and Canada: The Quest for Free Trade*. Washington, D.C.: Institute for International Economics, 1987.

———. "Merchandise Trade in the APEC Region: Is There Scope for Liberalization on an MFN Basis?" *The World Economy*, Special Issue on Global Trade Policy, 1995.

Wonnacott, Paul, and Ronald J. Wonnacott. "Liberalization in the Western Hemisphere: New Challenges in the Design of a Free-Trade Agreement." *North American Journal of Economics and Finance*, 1995.

Wonnacott, Ronald J. "Canada's Future in a World of Trade Blocs: A Proposal." *Canadian Public Policy,* vol. 1, Winter 1975a.

———. *Canada's Trade Options.* Ottawa: Economic Council of Canada, 1975b.

———. "Controlling Trade and Foreign Investment in the Canadian Economy: Some Proposals." *Canadian Journal of Economics,* vol. 15, November 1982.

———. "Canada and the U.S.-Mexico Free Trade Negotiations." Toronto: C. D. Howe Institute, 1990, Commentary 21.

Wonnacott, Ronald, and Paul Wonnacott. *Free Trade between the United States and Canada: The Potential Economic Effects.* Cambridge, Mass.: Harvard University Press, 1967.

World Bank. *East Asia and the Pacific Regional Development Review: Sustaining Rapid Development.* Washington, D.C.: World Bank, 1993.

Yeutter, Clayton K., and Warren H. Murayama. "A NAFTA for Europe." *Wall Street Journal,* May 19, 1995.

3
Regionalism and U.S. Trade Policy in Asia

Gary R. Saxonhouse

For more than twenty years, a firm U.S. commitment to existing multi-lateral trading institutions frustrated Australian and Japanese interest in regional trading arrangements in the Pacific Basin. In the mid-1980s, U.S. trade policy embraced regional trading arrangements as a tactic to promote a new round of multilateral trade negotiations. What began as a tactical ploy has now become an end in itself with the United States increasingly attempting to position itself at the center of a number of potentially important regional trading arrangements. This significant shift in U.S. trade policy has facilitated the formation of the Asia Pacific Economic Cooperation (APEC). Whether APEC will evolve into a full-fledged preferential trading arrangement remains to be seen.

Initial U.S. Interest in Preferential Trading Arrangements

The failure of the General Agreement on Tariffs and Trade (GATT) Ministerial in November 1982 to launch a new round of multilateral trade negotiations triggered a historically unprecedented U.S. interest in regional trade agreements. In 1983, the U.S. Trade Representative (USTR) commenced negotiations for bilateral preferential trading agreements (PTAs) with both Canada and Israel. These proposed bilateral trading arrangements marked a dramatic departure from the multilateralism that had been the cornerstone of U.S. trade policy for the preceding forty years. Howard Ellis (1945) spoke for U.S. economic policy makers in 1945 when he noted: "There are good reasons for believing that no device portends more restrictions of international trade in the postwar setting than bilateral trade arrangements."

Jagdish Bhagwati provided very helpful, detailed comments on the first draft of this chapter. He is in no way responsible for remaining errors in analysis and judgment.

In 1983, U.S. trade officials denied that these new regional trade initiatives meant any lessening of U.S. support for a multilateral trading system. Rather, foreshadowing now routine statements on trade policy, they argued that these initiatives would, first, put pressure on the reluctant contracting parties of the GATT to commence a new round of multilateral trade negotiations and, second, create more than enough new commercial opportunities for other American trading partners far outweighing the diversion of trade that might occur.[1]

In any event, the Reagan administration proclaimed at the time that this shift in trade policy was not meant to be parochial. The bilateral agreements with Canada and Israel were intended as a prelude to a worldwide search for new candidates for bilateral PTAs with the United States.[2]

Persistent U.S. Regionalism

Whether because of the incipient bilateralism of U.S. trade policy or otherwise, a new round of multilateral trade negotiations began under the framework of the Uruguay Round. Once started down the road to regionalism, however, U.S. trade policy makers have shown little inclination to turn back. Successive administrations have appeared ever more eager to use preferential trading arrangements as a critical element of trade policy *Realpolitik*. The European Community's grandiose plans to complete in 1992 what had begun in 1957 with the Treaty of Rome helped sway the Bush administration to do more than just agree to the ardent desire of President Salinas of Mexico to NAFTA-ize the U.S.-Canada Free Trade Agreement seriously. It also led the Bush administration to shelve the pretense of a worldwide search for new candidates for bilateral PTAs by making the extension of NAFTA to the rest of the Western Hemisphere its chief PTA objective.[3]

The Hawke Initiative

No sooner had the Bush administration expressed considerable interest in what would later be called the Enterprise for the Americas pref-

---

1. The first argument is distinguished as the "dynamic time path effect" by Bhagwati and Panagariya in chapter 1 of this volume. This effect is seen as benign by U.S. trade officials whereas Bhagwati and Panagariya consider this view to be unjustified. See also the theoretical treatment in Saxonhouse (1993a, 1993 b).
2. See the discussion in Bhagwati (1993).
3. See the discussion in ibid.

FIGURE 3–1
RELATIVE SIZE OF NOMINAL GROSS DOMESTIC PRODUCT, IN ASIA
AND THE WESTERN HEMISPHERE
(percent)

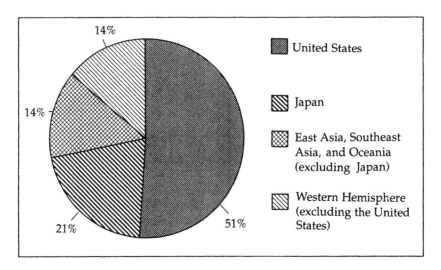

SOURCE: *United Nations Statistical Yearbook, 1994.*

erential trade area than the concern expressed outside the Western Hemisphere led it to reconsider its tactics. Burgeoning interest in the Hawke initiative for a Pacific trading arrangement, which had been announced by the Australian prime minister in January 1989 in Seoul without first consulting the United States, kindled fears in Washington that in tying itself closely to preferential trading relationships in the Western Hemisphere in response to EC 1992, the Bush administration ran the risk of triggering trade-diverting responses elsewhere in the Pacific Basin.[4] In the interest of improving access to economies elsewhere in the Western Hemisphere, there was concern that U.S. trade policy might ultimately impair access to far larger markets in East Asia and Oceania (see figures 3–1 and 3–2).

While the Bush administration, with its strong base in Texas, was unwilling to drop its plans for PTAs in the Western Hemisphere, par-

---

4. Consequences of the world's division into three preferential trading arrangements first began receiving theoretical treatment at this time. See, for example, Krugman (1991). More concrete discussion of this problem appears in Thurow (1992).

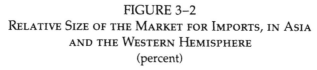

FIGURE 3–2
RELATIVE SIZE OF THE MARKET FOR IMPORTS, IN ASIA
AND THE WESTERN HEMISPHERE
(percent)

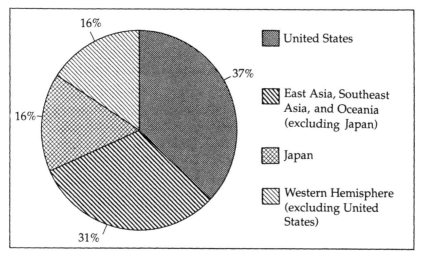

SOURCE: *United Nations Statistical Yearbook*, 1994.

ticularly one with Mexico, it was prepared to deal directly with some of the ill will that presidential candidate Bush's role in the passage of the Super-301-laden 1988 Trade Act had generated in East Asia.[5] In the first instance, the Bush administration wanted to ensure for itself a place at the conference table in Canberra for the founding of the Asia Pacific Economic Cooperation, which the Hawke initiative had inspired. To the satisfaction of the administration, APEC drew its membership from the Western Hemisphere as well as from East Asia and Oceania.[6] A year later, in a continuing effort to ensure that any PTA involving the western Pacific's major economies be pan-Pacific, Secretary of State James Baker, in Seoul at the second meeting of APEC, discouraged the formation of the exclusively Asian East Asian Eco-

---

5. The ramifications for the international economic system of the use of the various provisions of the Omnibus Trade and Competitiveness Act of 1988, but particularly Super 301, are discussed in Bhagwati and Patrick (1990).

6. APEC members include Australia, Brunei, Canada, Chile, China, Chinese Taipei, Hong Kong, Indonesia, Japan, Korea, Malaysia, Mexico, New Zealand, Papua New Guinea, the Philippines, Singapore, Thailand, and the United States.

nomic Group first proposed that same month by Malaysia's Prime Minister Mahathir. Ironically, Secretary Baker, who was then championing a trading arrangement in the Western Hemisphere that excluded extraregional members, was at the same time prepared to deny East Asia its own exclusive trading arrangement. Unable to stop its formation but assured of its exclusively consultative role, Secretary Baker was still able to prevent Japan and Korea from endorsing the Mahathir grouping (Saxonhouse 1993b, Petri 1993).

Conclusion of the Uruguay Round

The Bush administration left office in January 1993 unable to make the agreement with the European Union on agricultural subsidies that would permit the successful conclusion of the Uruguay Round. As negotiations dragged on through 1993, almost three years after the expected conclusion of the round, the Clinton administration, emulating the Reagan administration, sought to make tactical use of PTAs to drive further development of the multilateral trading system. In particular, the Clinton administration attempted to use the fortuitous timing of the NAFTA debate in the U.S. Congress and its sponsorship of the APEC Ministerial in Seattle in late 1993 to remind Europeans of the fragility of the multilateral approach to international trading relationships.

NAFTA, by itself, was too small to be of major concern to the Europeans. APEC, however, embraced economies that, in aggregate, had a gross domestic product in 1992 almost twice as large as the European Union (EU). (See table 3–1.) In an effort to give some enhanced visibility to APEC, whose accomplishments in its first four years of existence had been negligible, the Clinton administration convened an informal heads-of-state meeting following the formal APEC ministerial. More important, in a new departure, APEC's American-led Eminent Persons Group suggested that APEC be used as a framework within which free trade in the Asia-Pacific region might be achieved ("APEC Economic Leaders' Vision Statement" 1993).

Within weeks of the conclusion of the APEC Seattle meeting, seven and a half years of negotiations of the Uruguay Round ended in a far-reaching agreement. While there is no direct independent evidence to support the claim, many in APEC have been quick to suggest the successful Seattle meeting's influence on the outcome of these multilateral negotiations (Funabashi 1995, 107, 125).

A Pacific Preferential Trading Arrangement

After Seattle, as in the mid-1980s, whether or not the renewed interest evinced in PTAs was largely tactical, regionalism took on a life of its

GARY R. SAXONHOUSE

TABLE 3–1
REAL GROSS DOMESTIC PRODUCT AND POPULATION OF WORLD AND OF
MEMBERS OF MAJOR REGIONAL ECONOMIC ARRANGEMENTS, 1993

	Real Gross Domestic Product ($ trillion)	Population (billion)
World	23.0	5.50
APEC[a]	13.1	2.10
NAFTA[b]	7.3	0.37
AFTA[c]	0.4	0.33
CER[d]	0.4	0.02
EU[e]	7.3	0.37
MERCOSUR[f]	0.7	0.20

a. APEC: Australia, Brunei, Canada, Chile, China, Chinese Taipei, Hong Kong, Indonesia, Japan, Korea, Malaysia, Mexico, New Zealand, Papua New Guinea, Philippines, Singapore, Thailand, and the United States.
b. NAFTA: Canada, Mexico, and the United States.
c. AFTA: Brunei, Hong Kong, Indonesia, Malaysia, Philippines, Singapore, and Thailand.
d. CER (Closer Economic Relationship): Australia and New Zealand.
e. EU: Austria, Belgium, Denmark, Finland, France, Germany, Greece, Ireland, Italy, Luxembourg, Portugal, Sweden, and the United Kingdom.
f. MERCOSUR: Argentina, Brazil, Paraguay, and Uruguay.
SOURCE: Ministry of International Trade and Industry, *White Paper on International Trade* (Tokyo: 1995).

own for U.S. trade policy makers. The recommendations for trade liberalization made by the Eminent Persons Group in its initial report to the Seattle Ministerial were not accepted. Nevertheless, impressed by the seeming respect shown by the European Union for the potential economic consequences of an Asian-Pacific PTA, many Americans with an interest in trade policy, both in and out of government, were eager to maintain this arrangement as a viable option for APEC. The Clinton administration, however, faced indifference bordering on hostility on the part of the governments of most of the East Asian economies for any effort that would use APEC as the locus for negotiating preferential trade liberalization (Soesastro 1995).

The Clinton administration sought in early 1994 to counteract East Asian reluctance to use APEC as a negotiating body with yet another regional strategy. Instead of extending NAFTA exclusively southward as envisioned in the Bush administration's Enterprise for the Americas plan, the Clinton administration began discussing extending NAFTA

113

across the Pacific as well.[7] For example, as the *Nihon keizai shimbun* (May 3, 1994) speculated:

> South Korea and the U.S. have basically agreed that they will soon begin to take steps toward the signing of a free trade accord by 1996 or 1997 according to high-ranking Korean and U.S. officials.
>
> The bilateral arrangement is also designed to pave the way for South Korea to eventually join the U.S., Canada and Mexico in the North American Free Trade Agreement, the officials said. . . .
>
> American and Korean trade officials say they worked out the deal in late March through mid-April when U.S. Trade Representative Mickey Kantor met with South Korean Foreign Minister Han Sung Jo and other senior officials.
>
> The agreement was a result of each other's concessions trade officials said. The Seoul government agreed to the U.S. demand that agriculture and finance—potentially explosive issues at home—be included.

The ostensible purpose of such proposals was to reassure once more U.S. trading partners in East Asia and Oceania that the Clinton administration did not intend to draw a commercially restrictive line down the Pacific.[8] In common with the contemplated southward expansion, it was suggested that NAFTA's expansion across the Pacific might also take place on a country-by-country basis. A Singapore or a Korea might be paired with a Chile.

However speculative such suggestions by the Clinton administration might have been, they could only have been unsettling to APEC members outside the Western Hemisphere. In attempting to admit economies sequentially to NAFTA, U.S. trade policy would force its

---

7. See Manning and Stern (1994). Extending NAFTA across the Pacific was discussed as a trade policy option but not advocated in Bhagwati (1993).

8. The trade consequences for East Asia resulting from the formation of NAFTA have been estimated to be quite small. Primo Braga, Safadi, and Yeats 1994 estimate that NAFTA-induced trade diversion could cost East Asian economies between $380 million and $700 million. Losses would be concentrated in a few sectors, such as textiles, clothing, and ferrous metals, where high U.S. trade barriers exist. Such losses would be at the most .8 percent of East Asian exports to the United States. They would also be but 1 percent of the gains East Asia would receive from the successful implementation of the Uruguay Round agreements. While the Primo Braga-Safadi-Yeats findings, if anything, are an overestimate of the losses that might occur, their work does not address in a quantitative fashion the direct investment consequences of NAFTA's very restrictive rules of origin.

APEC trading partners to compete among themselves in granting concessions to avoid the trade-diverting and foreign investment–diverting consequences of late admission or even exclusion from an enlarged NAFTA.[9] The intent of such suggestions appeared to be less to reassure the East Asian trading partners of the United States about NAFTA and more to indicate that if APEC were to be excluded from the start as a framework for a pan-Pacific trading arrangement, the United States could clearly accomplish its regional trade diplomacy in less attractive ways from the East Asian point of view.[10]

Westward Expansion of NAFTA without Japan?

Is the threat of such a U.S. policy credible? Much depends on the ease of substitution between U.S. and Japanese capital, management, and technology in East Asian industry. It is highly unlikely that Japan would be the first East Asian economy asked to join NAFTA.[11] Unless Japan joins first, however, NAFTA's restrictive rules of origin will likely necessitate a greatly increased North American presence in the economy of the pioneer East Asian NAFTA members. As seen in figures 3–3 and 3–4, over the past decade Japan has been a much more significant source of direct investment in East Asia than have the United States and the European Union combined. And with the exception of investment in Hong Kong, much of this investment has been in manufacturing. Moreover, the greater part of that investment has been linked to export promotion as opposed to import-substituting activities (UNCTAD 1994; Tsushosangyosho 1994).

The past need not be a guide to the future. Figure 3–3 suggests

---

9. The scale of such diversion may be considerably less than is widely feared. While no modeling of a sequential trans-Pacific extension of NAFTA has been done, Brown, Deardorff, and Stern (1995) have looked at the growth of a trading bloc where Japan successively adds East Asian trading partners. Somewhat surprisingly, a Japan-Korea trading bloc imposes only $40 million in trade diversion on Taiwan and only a very small reduction in Taiwan's economic welfare. (Singapore actually experiences a small gain in economic welfare.) In common with Primo Braga-Safadi-Yeats, Brown-Deardorff-Stern make no effort to estimate investment or trade consequences. If a Korean-Japanese free trade area has so little consequence for Taiwan, perhaps the same would be true if Korea and the United States followed up on the alleged understanding reached between former USTR Mickey Kantor and former foreign minister Han Sung Jo.

10. See also the discussion in Funabashi (1995, 177).

11. See the discussion in Kuroda (1989) and in the United States International Trade Commission (1988).

FIGURE 3–3
DIRECT INVESTMENT FLOWS FROM JAPAN, THE UNITED STATES, AND THE EUROPEAN UNION TO EAST ASIA, 1985–1994
(billions of dollars)

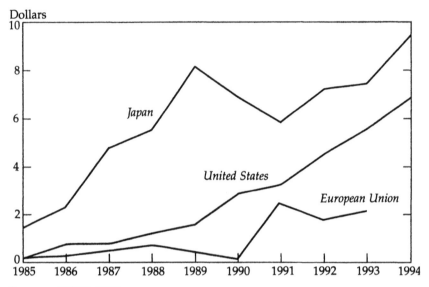

SOURCE: OECD, 1995.

that while U.S. direct investment in East Asia has lagged behind Japanese investment over this past decade, the past five years have witnessed significant increases. As table 3–2 makes clear, U.S. direct investment in East Asia, no less than Japanese investment, is heavily committed to manufacturing. Indeed, the U.S. and Japanese patterns of investment by industry are quite similar. The U.S. threat to expand NAFTA across the Pacific cannot be dismissed as entirely impractical.

The Bogor Declaration

Whatever role the threat of the westward expansion of NAFTA might have played in the discussions leading up to the ministerial and leaders meeting in Jakarta in November 1994, the basic stance of most East Asian members at that meeting toward using APEC to negotiate a pan-Pacific PTA did not appear to change markedly. The Bogor Declaration issued at the conclusion of the meeting calls for free trade in the region by 2020 with the agreement of more developed economies to complete their liberalization by 2010. Significantly, subject to these final dates,

116

FIGURE 3–4
INVESTMENT IN MANUFACTURING AS A PERCENTAGE OF TOTAL
ACCUMULATED DIRECT INVESTMENT BY JAPANESE COMPANIES, IN
SELECTED EAST ASIAN ECONOMIES, 1993

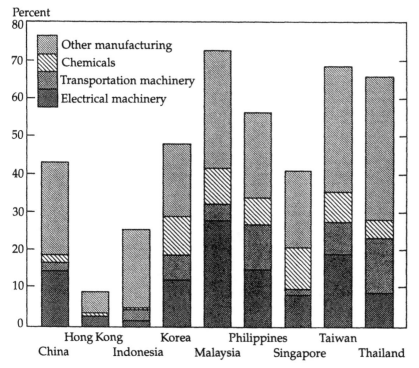

SOURCE: Okurasho, *Kokusai kinyu nenpo* (Tokyo: 1994).

the Bogor Declaration has left each APEC member free to decide the pace and terms of its liberalization. APEC members are committed to communicate with one another regularly on their progress and future plans for meeting the agreed upon final liberalization goal. In practice, this commitment has meant negotiations among APEC members on the form for such communication and the criteria by which trade liberalization can be evaluated. Interim benchmarks for member countries—for example, for tariff reduction, quota elimination, or any other kind of deregulation—have been scrupulously avoided.[12]

---

12. Unlike trade liberalization where the form and time path to achieve the agreed upon APEC goal is left entirely to the discretion of the members, collective action has been taken to draft a model APEC investment code. Such a code

117

TABLE 3–2
INVESTMENT IN MANUFACTURING AS PERCENTAGE OF TOTAL
ACCUMULATED DIRECT INVESTMENT IN SELECTED EAST ASIAN
ECONOMIES BY JAPANESE AND AMERICAN COMPANIES, 1993
(percent)

	Electrical Machinery		Transportation Machinery		Chemicals		Other Manufacturing	
	Japan	United States	Japan	United States	Japan	United States	Japan	United States
China	13.8	—	2.2	—	2.4	7.6	24.4	44.9
Hong Kong	2.5	14.9	—	—	0.3	1.4	5.6	9.1
Indonesia	1.6	—	2.7	—	10.4	1.2	20.7	2.0
Korea	11.7	6.2	6.9	2.0	10.0	7.1	18.9	25.9
Malaysia	27.4	44.5	4.6	—	9.3	2.5	31.2	8.9
Philippines	14.5	9.1	12.3	—	6.3	21.8	23.1	2.3
Singapore	8.0	21.3	1.6	—	10.5	6.0	20.5	25.4
Taiwan	18.9	25.0	8.3	—	8.2	25.9	32.9	10.3
Thailand	18.1	7.6	4.8	—	4.8	7.9	37.6	14.3

Empty cells = 0.
SOURCE: Okurasho, *Kokusai kinyu nenpo* (Yearbook of International Finance) (Tokyo, 1994); and United States Department of Commerce, *Survey of Current Business*, vol. 74, no. 8 (August 1994).

Europe's New Asian Trade Policy

While much of the regionalism in U.S. trade policy has been designed to cope with what are looked at on this side of the Atlantic as highly parochial trade policies by the European Union, Europe has responded with a new set of regional trade initiatives directed toward East Asia. Ironically, Europe has a long history of discriminating against East Asian products in general and Japanese products in particular.[13] It was

---

is designed to help free the flow of direct investment throughout the Pacific. It is not intended, however, that this code have the status of an international agreement. As adopted at the Jakarta Ministerial, the code has been designated as the APEC Nonbinding Investment Principles. As its name implies, it is supposed to encourage APEC members to liberalize their policies toward foreign investment but, at present, nothing more. See Soesastro (1995).

13. Saxonhouse (1992), using data from 1983, finds that Europe imports less from Japan than is predicted by a factor-endowment-based gravity equation. By contrast, the United States imports more than is predicted. Saxonhouse (1993b) finds that the results for Japan generalize to all the major East Asian

only in the 1970s that most of Western Europe stopped invoking GATT's Article XXXV against Japan.[14]

In recent years, economic relations between the European Union and East Asia have changed dramatically. As of the end of 1993, Japan had over $78 billion in direct investments in Europe (Okurasho 1994). Ninety-five percent of this investment has been made within the past ten years. At the same time, EU exports to Japan have grown fivefold, with EU exports to East Asia as a whole expanding fourfold (Tsusho-sangyosho 1994). Most significantly, the EU has made every effort to establish a distinct trade diplomacy with Japan. Despite the $60 billion in Japanese goods sold in the European Union and despite a $33 billion trade deficit with Japan, the EU has not supported U.S. trade policies toward Japan.[15] This diplomacy has been complemented by the Kaifu-Delors-Lubbers Declaration of Common Interests in July 1991 designed to elevate the EC-Japanese trading relationship to the status of the relationship that both maintain with the United States (*Nihon keizai shimbun*, July 27, 1991).

The Kaifu-Delors-Lubbers Declaration has since been generalized with the organization of the Asia-Europe Meeting (ASEM), which intends to bring together on a regular biennial schedule the leaders of ASEAN, China, the EU, Japan, and South Korea. The inaugural meeting in March 1996 in Bangkok announced the successful development of "a common vision for the future" and the forging of "a new comprehensive Asia-Europe Partnership for Greater Growth" (*Nihon keizai shimbun*, March 2, 1996).

TAFTA and the New Transatlantic Marketplace

Given the evident U.S. interest in establishing a preferential trading arrangement in the Pacific, EU interest in strengthening and renewing ties with East Asia is hardly surprising. More surprising, particularly in light of the stress by the leadership of the EU on the importance of

---

economies. These results are also consistent with the findings in Frankel and Wei (1995).

14. Article xxxv allows a contracting party to refuse to have its relations with another contracting party governed by the GATT.

15. Both Sir Leon Brittan and Jacques Santer, the current president of the European Union, have explicitly criticized U.S. trade policies toward Japan. Two days before the Clinton-Hosokawa Summit in February 1994, Sir Leon denounced U.S. demands that Japan agree to numerical targets for imports. In May and June of 1995, Sir Leon and President Santer criticized the United States for imposing sanctions on Japanese luxury automobiles without first seeking approval from the World Trade Organization.

maintaining and enhancing the role of the nascent World Trade Organization, was the 1995 proposal by Klaus Kinkel in Germany and other prominent European policy makers for the creation of a transatlantic free trade area (TAFTA). The TAFTA proposal was quickly, if cautiously, embraced by Secretary of State Christopher. Regional trading arrangements with non-European areas had first become part of U.S. trade policy as a tactic to encourage European participation in a new round of multilateral negotiations. By the spring of 1995, U.S. interest in preferential trade arrangements had come full circle with policy makers flirting with the notion that a PTA with Europe might possibly force a design of APEC more in accord with U.S. preferences.

As a serious proposal, TAFTA had an extremely short life span. Within a few months of its original conception, U.S. and EU officials announced that they were "not in a position to launch a full blown free trade area." The TAFTA proposal "raised many problems, including the need to make such a process compatible with World Trade Organization rules as well as its potential impact on various economic sectors" (*Business Times*, July 31, 1995). In place of TAFTA, U.S. and EU officials are now considering a more modest proposal for creating a new transatlantic marketplace (NTM). U.S. and EU officials envision the NTM as a forum for expanding ties between American and European government officials and business executives with an eye toward further eliminating trade barriers. At a summit meeting in December 1995, President Clinton, EU President Jacques Santer, and Spanish Prime Minister Felipe Gonzalez agreed to authorize a study by the newly created Transatlantic Business Dialogue (TABD) on ways to facilitate trade in goods and services between the United States and the EU and further reduce tariffs and nontariff barriers. As an interim objective, the hope was expressed that an agreement on the mutual recognition of product standards might be reached and that particular support be given to the efforts of the Organization for Economic Cooperation and Development to develop a comprehensive international investment code (U.S.–EU Action Plan" 1995).[16] Having hoped that the prospect of a TAFTA might push APEC to transform itself into a PTA, American officials are finding a formal PTA is no more feasible with the EU than it is with East Asia.

---

16. Since the Seville Summit, the TABD has played a role in promoting the new Information Technology Agreement (ITA). The ITA would eliminate all tariffs on information technologies by the year 2000 (*TABD Progress Report*, May 23, 1996).

APEC's East Asian Members and Reciprocity

U.S. trade policy of the past dozen years smacks more of Metternich than of John Stuart Mill. While U.S. policy may have successfully encouraged the launching of the Uruguay Round and may have helped bring it to a successful conclusion, it has also been successful in forming a preferential trading area in North America and in helping to promote APEC. The various twists and turns of U.S. trade policy thus far have not been successful, however, in encouraging the transformation of APEC into a pan-Pacific PTA. Whatever liberalization has thus far been stimulated by APEC, for example the initial market-opening plans announced at the 1995 APEC meeting in Osaka, has been framed on a WTO-consistent, unconditional most-favored-nation basis.

Why is it that most of APEC's East Asian members have been so resistant to the creation of a Pacific PTA? The American-led Eminent Persons Group arguing against unconditional MFN noted:

> Considerations suggest that, while APEC members should implement unilateral liberalization to the maximum extent possible, it will be expedient to pursue a strategy of negotiated liberalization as well. The largest members, including the United States, are unlikely to liberalize unilaterally when they can use the high value of access to their markets to obtain reciprocal liberalization from others. The same view applies to other economies in the region.
>
> The closely related consideration is that APEC as a whole is the world's largest trading region, considerably larger than even the EU. . . . the region would give away an enormous amount of leverage if its members . . . especially its largest members—were to liberalize unilaterally to any significant degree. (Asia Pacific Economic Cooperation 1994)

Unlike the United States, however, many of the East Asian APEC members see the commitment to free trade in the area by 2020 as little more than a commitment to continue the largely unilateral liberalization that has been continuing there for more than a decade. As can be seen from figure 3–5 and tables 3–3, 3–4, and 3–5, all the major economies in East Asia have undergone significant changes in their trade regimes, with substantial reductions in their nominal tariffs, their effective rates of protection, and their nontariff barriers. These changes in trade regime are not confined to East Asia. Table 3–5 shows that the Oceania APEC members, Australia and New Zealand, have also significantly reduced their protection for manufacturing over the past two decades.

From the perspective of East Asia and Oceania, unilateral liberal-

FIGURE 3–5
NOMINAL TARIFFS IN EAST ASIA, 1978, 1986, AND 1991

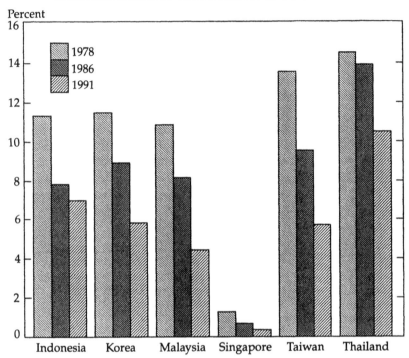

NOTE: Tariff rate = tariff revenues divided by imports.
SOURCE: IMF, *International Financial Statistics;* IMF Government Financial Statistics; Republic of China Ministry of Finance, Monthly Statistics of Exports & Imports.

ization has had quite tangible consequences. As seen in figure 3–6, over the past two decades trade liberalization in the major East Asian economies has been associated with rapid economic growth. East Asian liberalization of foreign investment rules is widely believed to have influenced economic growth by encouraging a rapid acceleration in the inflow of technology-enhancing, productivity-improving foreign direct investment (see figure 3–7). In East Asia, great emphasis has been placed on the role of foreign direct investment in stimulating economic growth despite, as seen in table 3–6, foreign direct investment's constituting a very small proportion of gross domestic capital formation in almost all these economies.

It is this confidence in the role that foreign direct investment can play in improving economic well-being that has led East Asian econo-

TABLE 3–3
EFFECTIVE RATES OF PROTECTION FOR MANUFACTURING IN EAST ASIA,
SELECTED YEARS, 1975–1992
(percent)

Korea		Thailand	
Year	Rate	Year	Rate
1980	21.9	1975	46.4
1983	19.6	1982	33.8
1985	10.7	1985	23.0
1990	5.8		

Malaysia			Indonesia		
Year	Textiles rate	Iron and steel rate	Year	Total manufacturing rate	Textiles rate
1982	29.2	24.6	1987	68	102
1985	17.4	10.7	1990	59	35
1987	7.9	2.2	1992	52	34

SOURCE: Sung-Duck Hong, Hyun-tai Kwak, "Changing Trade Policy and Its Impact on TFP in the Republic of Korea" *Developing Economies*, vol. 32, no. 4 (December 1994); Shujiro Urata and Kazuhiko Yokota, "Trade Liberalization and Productivity Growth in Thailand," *Developing Economies*, vol. 32, no. 4 (December 1994); Yumiko Okamoto, "Impact of Trade and Liberalization Policies on the Malaysian Economy," *Developing Economies*, vol. 32, no. 4 (December 1994); and P. G. Warr, "Comparative Advantage and Protection in Indonesia," *Bulletin of Indonesian Economic Studies*, vol. 28, no. 3 (December 1992).

mies to accelerate their removal of restrictions in the hope of attracting still more such investment. This liberalization of foreign investment restrictions, which has also motivated the liberalization of trade barriers, has been done unilaterally and competitively among the various East Asian economies (Soesastro 1996).

Given the stress that most of East Asia's APEC members have placed on liberalization and deregulation as a key element in their economic strategy, joining any arrangement that might in any way constrain their freedom of action is not a step taken lightly. Two considerations are particularly important. First, while joining a pan-Pacific PTA might aid in extracting market access concessions from nonmembers, such as the EU, the risk of failure is serious for APEC's East Asian members. As seen from figure 3–8, despite the high proportion of intra-APEC trade, its East Asian members' interests are fundamentally global. By itself, the European Union rivals the United States

TABLE 3–4

COVERAGE OF QUANTITATIVE RESTRAINTS ON IMPORTS AND
OTHER NONTARIFF BARRIERS, IN KOREA AND INDONESIA,
SELECTED YEARS, 1961–1990

(percent)

Korea-NTB Coverage		Indonesia-NTB Coverage	
Year	Percentage	Year	Percentage
1961	96	1986	43
1975	58	1987	25
1980	43	1988	21
1984	25	1989	15
1987	16	1990	13

SOURCE: Hyun-tai Kwak, "Changing Trade Policy and Its Impact on TFP in the Republic of Korea," *Developing Economies*, vol. 32, no. 4 (December 1994); General Agreements on Tariffs and Trade, *Trade Policy Review: Indonesia*, 1991 (Geneva 1991).

TABLE 3–5

EFFECTIVE RATE OF ASSISTANCE TO MANUFACTURING, INCLUDING
NONTARIFF BARRIERS, IN AUSTRALIA AND NEW ZEALAND,
SELECTED YEARS, 1970–1988

(percent)

Australia		New Zealand	
Year	Percentage	Year	Percentage
1970	35	1980	40
1980	22	1985	36
1990	17	1988	26

SOURCE: Industries Assistance Commission, *Annual Report 1987–1988* (Canberra: AGPS, 1988); W. Bates and G. White, *Industry Assistance Reform in New Zealand* (Wellington: New Zealand Government, 1988).

as a large market for East Asia. Second, as seen in table 3–7, as impressive as the liberalization of foreign direct investment undertaken to date has been, East Asian members of APEC have been reluctant to give up sovereignty in this area. They apparently wish to continue to control the pattern of liberalization no matter how fast the general pace may be (APEC 1995).

FIGURE 3-6
AVERAGE ANNUAL REAL GROWTH RATES, IN VARIOUS EAST ASIAN
COUNTRIES, 1970–1980 AND 1980–1993

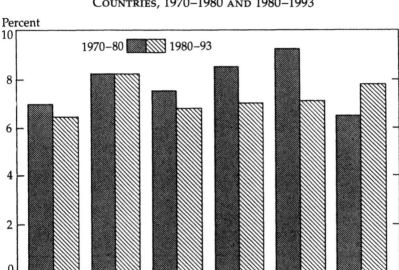

SOURCE: IMF, *International Financial Statistics.*

The Economics and Politics of Unilateral Liberalization

If in recent years economies in East Asia and Oceania have attempted
to pursue the liberalization of their foreign investment and trade regimes unilaterally and if these changes are viewed as highly successful,
is there any reason why they should now abandon those policies and
join a preferential trading arrangement?[17] A significant theoretical literature in economics bears on this question, at least insofar as trade is
concerned. As noted above, the report of the Eminent Persons Group,
in advocating what amounts to a PTA, stressed the argument that market power will make the PTA superior to unilateral liberalization because of terms-of-trade effects. This argument is at variance with the
traditional finding that for small countries facing exogenously determined prices joining a preferential trading arrangement is usually
dominated by unilateral liberalization (de Melo, Panagariya, and Ro-

17. The literature on this subject is surveyed in more detail and extended in
chapter 1 of this volume.

FIGURE 3–7
AVERAGE ANNUAL FOREIGN DIRECT INVESTMENT INFLOWS FOR VARIOUS
EAST ASIAN ECONOMIES, 1982–1992
(US $ millions)

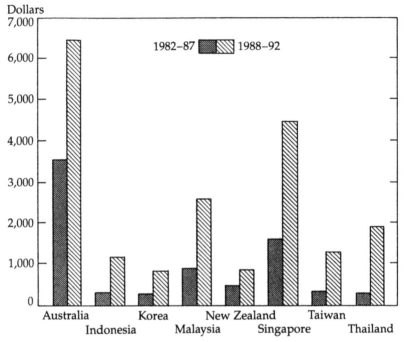

SOURCE: UNCTAD, *World Investment Report*, 1994.

drik 1993). The Eminent Persons Group presumably had in mind the case where, in the presence of another group of countries that maintain substantial protection, it can be welfare-enhancing for small countries to band together into a PTA in the interest of improving their terms of trade (Wonnacott and Wonnacott 1981; de Melo, Panagariya, and Rodrik 1993). The relevance of this particular case is questionable. As de Melo, Panagariya, and Rodrik note:

> If the world gets divided into inward-looking blocs, [unilateral trade liberalization] will become a less attractive option for countries outside the bloc than it is today. The [small] countries will then be better off, either seeking access to one of the blocs and adopting its trade policy or engaging in [regional integration] so as to promote freer trade among themselves. Of course, the current world being quite far from

126

TABLE 3–6
RATIO OF FOREIGN DIRECT INVESTMENT INFLOWS TO GROSS DOMESTIC
CAPITAL FORMATION AND RATIO OF GROSS DOMESTIC CAPITAL
FORMATION TO GDP IN EAST ASIA, 1981–1993
(percent)

Country	1981–1985	1986–1993
Australia	5.1	9.7
	(22.5)	(21.1)
Indonesia	1.0	3.0
	(25.0)	(29.5)
Korea	0.5	1.1
	(26.1)	(24.4)
Malaysia	10.8	14.8
	(32.9)	(24.9)
New Zealand	5.4	8.5
	(22.3)	(19.0)
Singapore	18.1	33.1
	(42.3)	(33.7)
Taiwan	1.5	3.0
	(24.1)	(18.0)
Thailand	3.2	5.6
	(22.7)	(21.4)

SOURCE: UNCTAD, *World Investment Report* 1994.

FIGURE 3–8
EAST ASIAN EXPORTS, EXCLUDING JAPAN, TO THE EUROPEAN UNION AND
THE UNITED STATES, 1981 AND 1991
(billions of dollars)

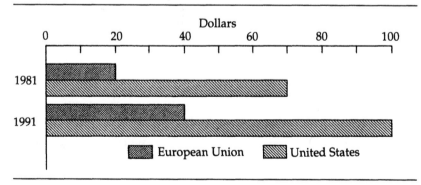

SOURCE: Tsushosangyosho, *Tsusho hakusho showa rokunen* (Tokyo: 1994).

127

TABLE 3–7
REMAINING RESTRICTIONS ON FOREIGN INVESTMENT MAINTAINED BY
EAST ASIAN APEC MEMBERS, 1995

Limitations on Foreign Ownership	*Tax Incentives*
China	China
Indonesia	Korea
Korea	Malaysia
Malaysia	Philippines
Philippines	Singapore
Singapore	Thailand
Taiwan	
Thailand	*Licensing*
	Brunei
Restricted Sectors	China
China	Indonesia
Indonesia	Korea
Malaysia	Malaysia
Philippines	Philippines
Singapore	Singapore
Taiwan	Taiwan
Thailand	Thailand
Performance Requirements	*Foreign Exchange Control*
China	China
Indonesia	Korea
Korea	Taiwan
Malaysia	
Philippines	*Restrictions on Land Ownership*
Taiwan	Brunei
Thailand	China
	Indonesia
	Philippines
	Taiwan
	Thailand

SOURCE: APEC, "Survey of Impediments to Trade and Investment in the APEC Regions," 1995.

consisting of closed blocs, the example does not justify a preference for [regional integration] over [unilateral trade liberal-
ization]. (de Melo, Panagariya, and Rodrik 1995)

Given that most of the economies of East Asia and Oceania view themselves as price takers, perhaps it is not surprising that they resist joining a PTA.

The trade models just referenced abstract from political considerations. The political decision on whether to join a PTA has also been modeled.[18] An important strand of this literature treats interest groups as participants in a competition for political favors that are meted out by politicians each serving his or her own selfish interest (Grossman and Helpman 1995). This competition is part of one of two distinct stages of strategic interaction in the decision-making process. One of these stages is domestic and the other international; neither stage can be analyzed without the other. As Grossman and Helpman note, "International interdependence sets the parameters for the domestic political context, while the domestic political environment constrains the actions that governments can take internationally" (Grossman and Helpman 1995). Unsurprisingly, analysis of such processes finds that the conditions that would make it politically possible for a country to join a PTA are often the same conditions that make it economically disadvantageous (for example, large trade diversions).

Unilateral trade liberalization, by definition, is unconstrained by the demands of international reciprocity. If getting political support for joining a PTA may result in an outcome detrimental to a country's economic interest, unilateral trade liberalization could also be consistent with developing significant support for liberal trade. The absence of foreign constraints is not inevitably a problem for political leaders who seek to build a constituency for economic liberalization. Foreign demands for liberalization can be useful in breaking apart recalcitrant domestic coalitions (for example, *gaiatsu*, that is, foreign pressure on Japan). Alternatively, such demands can be economically and politically unreasonable (as, for example, demands for voluntary import expansions have been on some occasions). Even under conditions where joining a PTA might offer more in the way of export opportunities than unilateral trade liberalization, in some instances East Asian trade policy makers may do better for the welfare of their economies by having the freedom to design liberalization packages facing only domestic constraints. This, in fact, is the conclusion many East Asian policy makers have reached.

U.S. Views on East Asian Liberalization

At least part of the impatience of U.S. trade negotiators with the unwillingness of most other APEC members to join a PTA stems from a different perception of the liberalization process there. The report of the Eminent Persons Group remarks in its critique of unilateral liberaliza-

---

18. See once again the critical survey of this literature in Bhagwati and Panagariya, chapter 1 in this volume.

TABLE 3–8
EAST ASIAN BILATERAL TRADE SURPLUSES, 1992
(billions of dollars)

Region	United States	European Union
East Asia	98	58
East Asia (excluding Japan)	42	25

SOURCE: Tsushosangyosho, *Tsusho hakusho rokunen* (Tokyo, 1994).

tion that "effective protection remains high in the region despite the liberalization" (APEC 1994). The very large bilateral trade surpluses (see table 3–8) that most of the East Asian economies maintain with most of their nonoil trading partners are viewed not as an indication of thrift but wrongly as the product of onerous trade barriers.[19]

For example, U.S. trade policy makers have been too preoccupied with Japan's trade surpluses to appreciate the extraordinary changes that have occurred in the Japanese economy.[20] Despite the endless bilateral negotiations with the United States, Japan instituted the vast majority of those changes in the regulation of its economy because it was in Japan's own economic interest to do so. The U.S. refusal to acknowledge Japan's liberalization may well be repeated elsewhere. Indeed, the Clinton administration has rationalized its aggressive unilateral policy toward Japan by the need to show the rest of East Asia that the United States will not tolerate any emulation of Japan's "restrictive policies."

Osaka and the Future of APEC

The willingness of American trade negotiators in the spring of 1995 to ignore WTO dispute resolution procedures has undercut whatever chance there might have been that most East Asian members of APEC would agree to enter into formal negotiations for a PTA under the auspices of WTO's Article XXIV. It is now widely believed in East Asia that the best protection against U.S. unilateralism is the EU, the one significant economic grouping excluded from APEC.

---

19. These very large bilateral trade imbalances made it unlikely that the United States could conclude a preferential trading arrangement with East Asia even if the majority of East Asian economies were so inclined. See Grossman and Helpman (1995).

20. Some evidence on this is provided in Saxonhouse (1993c, 1994a, and 1994 b, particularly table 5).

Given that an informal consensus appears to have been reached at Osaka that no attempt will be made in the foreseeable future to notify the WTO under Article xxiv that a preferential trading arrangement is being negotiated, any APEC liberalization not offered on an unconditional MFN basis to all WTO members will be a violation of the WTO's Article I.[21] In consequence, the comprehensive liberalization plans to be presented by APEC members at the Manila APEC Ministerial in 1996 or at the 1997 APEC in Canada are expected to be framed as unconditional MFN. For the foreseeable future, liberalization plans are unlikely to give special preference to imports from fellow APEC members.

In addition to the apparent consensus that there will be no APEC negotiations under WTO provisions governing PTAs, another informal consensus reached at Osaka holds that any formal WTO-style negotiations at all should be avoided. In the months before the Osaka Ministerial and Leaders meeting, American negotiators had hoped to get an agreement that APEC member liberalization plans when finally offered would be strictly comparable with one another. With acceptance of the principle of strict comparability, formal negotiations would almost inevitably have followed. In its final version, however, the action agenda adopted at Osaka committed members only "to endeavor to insure the overall comparability of their trade and investment liberalization and facilitation."

The same desire to avoid formal negotiations is also behind the consensus reached at Osaka on how to combine comparability of liberalization with the very diverse circumstances of APEC members. In particular, Japan, China, Taiwan, and Korea have all been eager that APEC's action agenda allow for special treatment of sensitive sectors, such as agriculture.

U.S. negotiators have opposed such special treatment, arguing that it is inconsistent with the Bogor Declaration's commitment to free trade in the Asia-Pacific area by 2020. U.S. opposition has not been sufficient to prevent the APEC Action Agenda from agreeing that "given the diverse circumstances in the APEC economies flexibility will be available in dealing with issues arising from such circumstances in the liberalization and facilitation process." Many East Asian members of APEC understand the adoption of this language to mean that free trade in the Asia-Pacific area by 2020 does not necessarily mean

---

21. The decision at Osaka to disband the Eminent Persons Group, which had been forcefully pushing for liberalization based on conditional MFN, is symbolic of this new consensus.

zero tariffs in all sectors by 2020, according to *Nihon keizai shimbun*, November 24, 1995.

Finale

The outcome of thirteen years of U.S. pursuit of regional trade policies could possibly be a network of preferential trade arrangements centered on the United States. If the U.S. experience in Asia is any guide, a more likely outcome is an increasingly strengthened multilateral system based on the WTO. Given the experience of the U.S.-Japan auto parts dispute in the spring of 1995, many in East Asia believe that the best hope for parrying U.S. pressure is in the WTO, where the EU maintains a substantial balancing presence. The EU is willing to play this role because of its interest in the growing economic opportunities in East Asia and because of its suspicions of U.S. bilateralism.[22] As if to underline the overwhelming primacy of WTO obligations, the APEC meeting in Osaka has effectively rejected the recommendation of the Eminent Persons Group for a dispute mediation service and agreed only to "examine the possible future evolution of [APEC dispute settlement procedures]."[23] According to a clear consensus reached at Osaka, nothing should be done that would in any way undercut the WTO's newly strengthened dispute settlement mechanism.

What began as *Realpolitik* may well end up conforming to the visions of Immanuel Kant and Woodrow Wilson. The U.S. plunge into PTAs may be leading instead to a much stronger, broadly based multilateral system, whatever current U.S. government preferences might be. A stronger WTO may prove capable of constraining even its most powerful members. The international economic transactions of even the countries that need the system the least in the short run may come to be strictly governed by international law. This outcome is certainly in the long-term interest of the United States.

References

"APEC Economic Leaders' Vision Statement." *U.S. Department of State Dispatch*, vol. 4, November 29, 1993, pp. 833–34.

---

22. In other contexts in the WTO, the United States plays a similar balancing role vis-à-vis the EU, a fact apparently also widely appreciated in East Asia.

23. See APEC 1995. Already at the Jakarta Ministerial in 1995, the Eminent Persons Group proposed a dispute resolution mechanism in connection with the APEC nonbinding investment principles. Fearing American domination, western Pacific APEC members preferred arbitration procedures consistent with members' existing international commitments.

Asia Pacific Economic Cooperation. "Foreign Direct Investment and APEC Economic Integration." *APEC* 95-EC-01, 1995.

———. "Survey of Impediments to Investment and Trade in the APEC Region." *APEC* 95-CT-01.2, 1995.

———. "Milestones in APEC Liberalizations: A Map of Market Opening Measures by APEC Economics," 1995.

———. *Achieving the APEC Vision: Second Report of the Eminent Persons Group.* Singapore: APEC, 1994.

———. *Implementing the APEC Vision: The Third Report of the Eminent Persons Group.* Singapore: APEC, 1995.

Bhagwati, Jagdish. "NAFTA: Clinton's Trading Choices." *Foreign Policy*, Summer 1993.

Bhagwati, Jagdish, and Hugh Patrick, eds. *Aggressive Unilateralism: America's 301 Trade Policy and the World Trading System.* Ann Arbor, Mich.: University of Michigan Press, 1990.

Brown, Drusilla K., Alan V. Deardorff, and Robert M. Stern. "The Economic Effects of an East Asian Trading Bloc." Research Forum on International Economics Discussion Paper no. 381, 1995.

Business Times. July 31, 1995.

de Melo, Jaime, Arvind Panagariya, and Dani Rodrik. "The New Regionalism: A Country Perspective." In Jaime de Melo and Arvind Panagariya, eds., *New Dimensions in Regional Integration.* Cambridge: Cambridge University Press for the World Bank and CEPR, 1995.

Ellis, Howard S. "Bilateralism and the Future of International Trade." *Essays in International Finance*, vol. 5, Summer 1945.

Frankel, Jeffrey, and Shang-Jin Wei. "The New Regionalism and Asia: Issues and Impacts." Paper presented at the Conference on the Emerging Global Trading Environment and Developing Asia, Manila, May 29–30, 1995.

Funabashi, Yoichi. *Asia Pacific Fusion: Japan's Role in APEC.* Washington, D.C.: Institute for International Economics, 1995.

Grossman, Gene, and Elhanan Helpman. "The Politics of Free Trade Agreements." *American Economic Review*, vol. 85, September 1995.

Krugman, Paul R. "Is Bilateralism Bad?" In Elhanan Helpman and Assaf Razin, eds., *International Trade and Trade Policy.* Cambridge, Mass.: MIT Press, 1991.

Kuroda, Makoto. "Strengthening Japan-U.S. Cooperation and the Concept of Japan-U.S. Free Trade Arrangements." In Jeffrey J. Schott, ed., *Free Trade Areas and U.S. Trade Policy.* Washington, D.C.: Institute for International Economics, 1989.

Manning, Robert A., and Paula Stern. "The Myth of the Pacific Community. *Foreign Affairs*, November–December 1994.

Nihon Keizai Shimbun (Japan economic journal). July 27, 1991.

———. November 24, 1995.

———. March 2, 1996.

Okurasho. *Kokusai Kinyu Nenpo* (yearbook of international finance). Tokyo, 1994.

Petri, Peter. "The East Asian Trading Bloc: An Analytical History." In Jeffrey A. Frankel and Miles Kahler, eds., *Regionalism and Rivalry: Japan and the U.S. in Pacific Asia.* Chicago: University of Chicago Press and the National Bureau of Economic Research, 1993.

Primo Braga, Carlos A., Raed Safadi, and Alexander Yeats. "NAFTA's Implications for East Asian Exports." World Bank Policy Working Paper no. 1351, 1994.

Saxonhouse, Gary R. "Europe's Economic Relations with Japan." In William James Adams, ed., *Singular Europe.* Ann Arbor, Mich.: University of Michigan Press, 1993.

———. "Pricing Strategies and Trading Blocs in East Asia." In Jeffrey Frankel and Miles Kahler, eds., *Regionalism and Rivalry: Japan and the U.S. in Pacific Asia.* Chicago: University of Chicago Press for the National Bureau of Economic Research, 1993a.

———. "Trading Blocs and East Asia." In Jaime de Melo and Arvind Panagariya, eds., *New Dimensions in Regional Integration.* Cambridge, Mass.: Cambridge University Press, 1993b.

———. "What Does Japanese Trade Structure Tell Us about Japanese Trade Policy?" *Journal of Economic Perspectives,* vol. 7, Summer 1993c.

———. "The Economics of the U.S.-Japan Framework Talks." *Hoover Essays in Public Policy,* vol. 53, October 1994a.

———. "The 1994 Economic Report of the President and Japan." Research Seminar in International Economics Discussion Paper no. 387, 1994b.

Soesastro, Hadi. "The APEC Nonbinding Investment Principles." *NBR Analysis,* vol. 6, April 1995.

———. *Policies of Asian Developing Countries towards Direct Investment.* Jakarta: Center for Strategic and International Studies, 1996.

Tabd Progress Report. May 23, 1996.

Thurow, Lester C. *Head to Head.* New York: Murrow, 1992.

Tsushosangyosho. *Tsusho Hakusho Showa Rokunen* (International Trade & Industry white paper). Tokyo, 1994.

UNCTAD. *World Investment Report.* New York: United Nations, 1994.

"U.S.-EU Action Plan Includes Broad Agenda." *Inside U.S. Trade,* vol. 13, November 1, 1995.

U.S. International Trade Commission. *Pros and Cons of Initiating Negotiations with Japan to Explore the Possibility of a United States-Japan Free Trade Area Agreement: Report to the Senate Finance Committee.* Washington, D.C.: Government Printing Office, 1988.

Wonnacott, Paul, and Ronald Wonnacott. "Is Unilateral Tariff Reduction Preferable to a Customs Union? The Curious Case of the Missing Foreign Tariff." *American Economic Review,* vol. 71, September 1981.

4
Regionalism and U.S. Trade Policy
Claude E. Barfield

This chapter argues that the United States, alone among the major trading powers, holds a strong, balanced trade and investment position in each of the major regional economic areas. Thus, because its economic interests span the global trading world, the goals of U.S. trade and investment policy are best achieved through the multilateral trading system and embodied in the new World Trade Organization. This being the case, the decision of the Clinton administration to give equal priority to regional preferential trading agreements is a mistake. Contrary to the views of most of the Washington trade policy community, the deferment until 1997 of action in regional trade negotiations will be beneficial if it allows opponents of preferential trading arrangements in Latin America and Asia to strengthen their position against reciprocity-based free trade agreements.

The United States—World Trader and Investor

In assessing the comparative positions of the three leading world trading regions—Asia, the United States, and the European Union—there are two paradoxical circumstances to keep in mind regarding the United States. First, to a greater extent than either of the other leading powers, the United States is in the position to be a major player in all regions because of its trade and investment patterns. Europe is much less involved in Japan and Asia than are either the United States or the Asian economies, and Asia, in turn, is much less involved in Europe than is the United States. In addition, the historically and currently strong position of the United States in Central and South America underscores U.S. prominence as the only truly worldwide economic power and player with strong ties in every important economic region.

A second paradox is that, because of its huge internal market and abundant natural resources, the United States is much less dependent on trade than is either of its major rivals. Exports and imports accounted for only 11 to 18 percent of U.S. GDP during the 1980s, while the comparable figures for the European Union were between 45 and 47 percent, and for Asia, between 26 and 29 percent (for developing Asia, between 37 and 47 percent; Anderson and Norheim 1993).

World Trade and Investment Ties. Table 4–1 sets out the trade patterns of the EU, North America, and East Asia from 1980 to 1991. It is clear from the table that the trade relations between North America and East Asia are much stronger than those between the EU and the other two regions. Furthermore, only North America demonstrated reasonably strong relations with both of the other regions. For instance, in 1991, the EU and East Asia respectively accounted for 17.3 and 22.7 percent of total North American trade. The EU, however, accounted for only 14.2 percent of East Asian trade; conversely, East Asia accounted for only 7 percent of EU trade. A recent projection suggests that by the year 2003, U.S. trade with East Asia will be twice that with Europe (Noland 1995).

In absolute terms, U.S.–East Asian trade has exceeded U.S.–EU trade since the early 1980s: in 1993, total U.S.–European trade was $235 billion, while total U.S.–East Asian trade was $347 billion (U.S. Department of Commerce, Foreign Trade Highlights 1993). Furthermore, as table 4—2 indicates, East Asian countries remain highly dependent on the U.S. economy as a market for their exports. The United States ranks either first or second as an export outlet for each of them except China. Using data that include Hong Kong's reexports as Chinese exports, Chinese exports jumped $21 billion to more than 28 percent of China's global exports (Korea Economic Institute of America 1994, 205).

U.S.–European Investment Ties. In a world where interdependence is increasingly defined by investment and not by trade flows, the enduring strong ties between the United States and Europe must be factored into any analysis of regional economic relations. And here the picture is quite the reverse of developing trade patterns. Jointly, the United States and Europe control more than two-thirds of all foreign direct investment, with total cross-investment in each other's economy of $488 billion.

In 1990, European companies accounted for 64 percent of all foreign direct investment in the United States, while 44 percent of total U.S. foreign direct investment was in Europe. In contrast, Asia accounts for about 20 percent of foreign investment in the United States and about 16 percent of U.S. foreign direct investment (Barfield 1992). In 1993, the total value of Japan's investment in Europe was just over $75 billion—this contrasted with a total U.S. cumulative investment of almost $240 billion (Noland 1995).

137

TABLE 4–1
TRADE PATTERNS OF THE EUROPEAN UNION, NAFTA, AND ASIA, 1983–1993
(percent)

Year	1983	1984	1985	1986	1987	1988	1989	1990	1991	1992	1993
EU											
EU	52.9	52.5	53.5	56.8	58.2	58.6	58.5	59.2	59.7	60.2	54.7
NAFTA	9.4	10.3	10.5	9.6	9.1	8.9	8.9	8.4	8.3	8.1	8.9
ASIA	3.8	3.9	4.1	4.3	4.6	4.9	5.0	4.9	5.4	5.7	7.1
NAFTA											
EU	18.0	16.9	17.7	18.7	19.4	18.3	17.8	19.3	18.8	18.0	15.9
NAFTA	36.6	37.5	38.0	35.6	35.6	35.8	36.2	36.9	37.2	37.9	40.2
ASIA	12.7	12.6	12.0	12.9	14.5	15.4	15.5	15.3	16.2	17.0	17.4
ASIA											
EU	12.7	12.0	12.4	14.1	14.2	14.1	13.8	14.9	14.4	14.1	13.9
NAFTA	21.4	22.8	22.0	22.9	22.7	22.1	21.6	20.2	19.1	18.9	19.0
ASIA	24.2	24.7	25.6	25.3	27.1	28.7	30.1	31.9	34.6	36.7	36.5

NOTE: EU includes the twelve member countries; NAFTA includes Canada, Mexico, and the United States; Asia includes a total of thirty-five countries.
SOURCE: International Monetary Fund data are from *Directory of Trade Statistics*, 1990, 1994.

TABLE 4–2
Snapshot of the Big Emerging Markets, 1994
($ billions)

Big Emerging Markets	Total Imports, 1993	U.S. Market Share (%), 1993	Projected Total Imports, 2010
Chinese economic area	320	11	577
Indonesia	29	14	97
India	24	12	79
South Korea	84	18	236
Mexico	49	85	119
Argentina	17	22	28
Brazil	26	23	69
South Africa	20	14	36
Poland	16	6	18
Turkey	29	11	67

Source: U.S. Department of Commerce, *Business America, 1994.*

The Clinton Trade Policy and Its Critics

The 1994 and 1995 Economic Reports of the President present detailed explanations of the Clinton administration's goals and priorities for trade policy. They represent a distillation of the strongly held views of the administration's principal economic spokespersons on trade—National Economic Council Chair Laura Tyson and Under Secretary of the Treasury Lawrence Summers.

While acknowledging that the "most far reaching of the administration's market opening efforts has been . . . the Uruguay Round of GATT," the 1995 *Economic Report* states that the "most distinctive legacy" of the Clinton administration in the trade policy arena will be the "foundation it has laid for the development of overlapping plurilateral trade agreements as stepping stones to global free trade."

This should come as no surprise, because Summers, before joining the Clinton administration, had forcefully stated his "press on all fronts," pro–trade bloc philosophy. He stated in 1991:

Economists should maintain a strong, but rebuttable, presumption in favor of all lateral reductions in trade barriers, whether they be multi, uni, bi, tri, or plurilateral. Global liberalization may be best, but regional liberalization is very likely to be good. (Panagariya 1995)

The administration is also candid about the underlying mercantilist goals that drive the new thrust of U.S. trade policy. In describing

139

Clinton trade policy last year, the 1994 *Economic Report* stated: "The administration's trade policy can be described as 'export activism.' " "Export activism" also is at the heart of the Clinton regional initiatives, as the 1995 *Economic Report* makes clear when it notes that "Export and investment opportunities in emerging markets in Latin America and Asia will be a key engine of growth for the U.S. economy over the next decade."

Together, the 1994 and 1995 Economic Reports of the President also set forth the case for regional trading arrangements as building blocks toward multilateral free trade. First, the administration argues that regional trading agreements allow some trading nations to move forward faster and achieve deeper economic integration than do cumbersome multilateral negotiations that include more than 120 nations.

Second, the administration predicts that a "self-reinforcing process" will be put in place in which, as the free trade area expands, it will become increasingly attractive to outsiders who will clamor to become member countries.

Finally, the administration sets out its own definition of open regionalism (a definition that largely tracks that of the APEC Eminent Persons Group). In committing itself to open regionalism, the Clinton administration states that it will negotiate only regional agreements that are nonexclusive and open to new members to join, and that it will require that such agreements adhere to the GATT Article XXIV rule, which prohibits an increase in average external barriers (for comments on this rule see below, in the section on WTO). Most important, though not stated explicitly, the Economic Report assumes that regional agreements will extend benefits to outsiders only on a conditional MFN basis.

The Dissenters. Even before the Clinton administration moved to bring regional preferential agreements to the forefront of U.S. trade policy, some foreign observers, particularly promarket Europeans, had expressed alarm at the potential consequences of a U.S. drift away from multilateralism. In 1989, Martin Wolf, then the director of research for the Trade Policy Research Center in London, had stated:

> The fundamental issue . . . is why the United States has abandoned well over half a century of adherence to the unconditional MFN principle and now sees discrimination as a solution to its trading woes. . . . Historically, FTAs have been the economic policy of the weak. [For instance], the discriminatory policies of the EU have their roots not only in fear of competition (initially from the United States, now from the Far East) but also in the limited number of instruments of

foreign policy available to it. Should one interpret the movement of the United States in the 1980s toward a trade policy based on discrimination as a tacit admission of its relative economic and political decline? The answer, unfortunately, is yes.

And he warned:

The shift in U.S. thinking towards FTAs, and more generally toward bilateralism as a principle, rather than a shamefaced expedite, is momentous. As the progenitor and most enthusiastic upholder of the unconditional-most-favored-nation principle, the United States may well doom the GATT system in its present form by this defection. (Wolf 1989)

More recently, other economists have expanded and deepened the critique of the Clinton administration's move to give top priority to negotiating preferential trading arrangements around the world. Taking issue with the administration's assertions regarding the positive benefits of regional and bilateral free trade pacts, these dissenters begin by taking the argument back to the fundamental fact that, in the words of Jagdish Bhagwati, it is "folly" to equate "free trade areas (FTAs) with free trade" because "they are inherently preferential and discriminatory."[1]

In building a case against a proliferation of free trade agreements, Anne Krueger focuses particularly on the potentially damaging political economy consequences of rules of origin (ROOs). Rules of origin are border measures in FTAs to ensure that trade diversion does not occur, allowing countries outside the FTA to transship goods among FTA members. ROOs consist of negotiated domestic content requirements.

FTA negotiations allow producer groups among the member nations to lobby for increased protection as a payoff for their support of the proposed agreement. ROOs negotiations result in a maze of regulations (in NAFTA there are 200 pages devoted to ROOs), and they often result in increased protection. In a recent study describing U.S. and EU manipulation of rules of origin in such sectors as automobiles, semi-

---

1. I do not propose in the text of this chapter to treat in detail the evolution of economic theory and empirical research regarding customs unions and free trade areas—I shall refer the reader to the excellent collection of papers in Anderson and Blackhurst (1993) and de Melo and Panagariya (1994). This chapter will only partially map this terrain by explaining the particular points chosen by Bhagwati, Krueger, and other economists who have raised questions specifically about the Clinton administration's decision to give top priority to regional trading arrangements (Bhagwati and Krueger 1995).

conductors, textiles, and television screens, trade analyst Jeri Jensen-Moran concluded:

> Rather than the . . . technical tools they were meant to be, ROOs in key economic sectors can instead operate as industrial policy. . . . In effect, rules of origin become vehicles of forced investment, facing companies located outside the free trade area with a stark choice: invest in production facilities within the region, or don't trade with it at all. The resulting investment provides high-wage jobs and technology to the locality, but it also distorts trade and investment patterns and undermines the long-term competitiveness of the companies and countries involved. (Jensen-Moran 1995)

Further, a world of increasing FTAs, with numerous ROOs, adds to the possibility that individual nations will begin to exploit the system with little regard for logic or systemwide rules. For example, the United States already maintains contradictory positions regarding automobile transplants and ROOs—demanding that autos from Japanese U.S. transplants not be counted as U.S. exports to Japan, while at the same time vigorously protesting an EU proposal to define these cars as Japanese under their VER quota with Japan.

FTAs must also be judged in light of the increased use of antidumping and other so-called unfair trade practice measures as instruments of protection. As Bhagwati has noted in several papers, administered protection is highly selective, and it is likely that when they face major adjustment problems resulting from lowered barriers, FTA members will lash out against nonmember suppliers with antidumping suits or other protectionist devices. Bhagwati's hypothetical case can be strengthened with recent history—both Mexico and Canada are pressing the United States to exclude them from administered protection actions. The Canadian trade minister has argued, for instance, that for steel and automobile parts North America should be considered one market, and therefore it makes no sense to mount antidumping suits against Canadian companies in these sectors. In addition, the EU has eliminated antidumping cases against countries in European free trade areas (EFTAs) and the European Economic Area; and there are calls by other eastern European countries for the EU to adopt the same policy for this region in future trade negotiations.

More broadly, the critics point out that FTAs dominated by one economy (NAFTA and its extension, for instance) allow the large economy to extract concessions that it could not get from full multilateral negotiations. Here again recent events support the hypothetical case. The Clinton administration is determined to force the inclusion of environmental and labor standards in extensions of NAFTA—and indeed, while it has never explicitly stated such a position regarding APEC, it has made clear that new presidential trade negotiating authority must include the power to conclude environmental and labor agreements. This being the case, those APEC nations who fear that the United States might well in the future attempt to impose its labor and environmental views in a trade treaty have reason for disquiet.

There is, finally, one other aspect of U.S. regional trade policy that the countries of Asia and South America (and even the EU) should consider. Though there is little evidence that the United States is proceeding by any grand design, the current plans to proceed separately with U.S.-centered regional trade agreements both in the Pacific and in Latin America will give substantially larger benefits to the United States than to any of the other countries in the regions. This situation would be greatly compounded should the EU follow through on recent calls for a North Atlantic Free Trade Agreement. In the most expansive projection, the United States could be the single hub in a three-spoked trade wheel, with favored access to most of the markets in Latin America, East Asia, and Europe, while no other country would enjoy anything like this status. Such a scenario is unlikely, but it is a logical extension of U.S. policy today, and it should give other nations pause for consideration (see the Wonnacot chapter in this volume for more details on the trade-offs of hub-and-spoke systems). Only a multilateral negotiation holds the potential of equalizing benefits across regions and national boundaries.

Multiple FTAs and the Practical World of Negotiations

Broadening the analysis from the analytical realm of economists to the practical world of the trade negotiators, further reasons can be advanced for skepticism regarding the Clinton administration's enthusiasm for a world of multiple FTAs. First, though, it is necessary to challenge directly the premise that multilateral negotiations are necessary because the WTO has become so large (120-plus nations) and unwieldy that multilateral negotiations are unmanageable and would go on forever without resolution. Here, the example of the eight-year Uruguay Round negotiations is always invoked. But in reality, the Uruguay Round demonstrated something very different from this now conventional wisdom. The large majority of small and developing countries were ready for an agreement long before the two superpowers—the United States and the EU—could reconcile their differences. What delayed the conclusion of the Uruguay Round was the clash between these two negotiating teams (on agriculture, entertainment, and telecommunications), not the fact that consensus had to be reached with more than 100 other nations.

In addition to the fact that from both an efficiency and equity point of view, multilateral agreements are clearly preferable, there are also quite practical negative consequences of a move toward a world of multiple bilateral and multilateral trading arrangements. First, the effort and resources that will have to be devoted to negotiating such agreements will inevitably divert attention and resources from the immensely complicated task of substantively carrying out the mandates of the Uruguay Round and administratively getting the WTO running efficiently and smoothly.

Second, a trading world dotted with separate bilateral and multilateral FTAs, each with different interim timetables, tariff levels, and nontariff barrier liberalization rules, would become enormously inefficient. Assuming that most of the existing and proposed multilateral agreements come into existence, a multinational corporation such as IBM, Siemens, or Samsung would face a daunting task in sorting out trade rules that governed their simultaneous operations in APEC, NAFTA, MERCOSUR, the European Economic Area—not to mention individual countries such as Chile or Turkey, which had separate arrangements with regional groupings and individual nations.

A vision of this dubious "spaghetti bowl" world of overlapping free trade areas is presented in a recent paper by economists Paul and Ronald Wonnacott (Wonnacott and Wonnacott 1995). The Wonnacott chapter in this volume presents a variation of their original proposal. Both researchers are dedicated to the multilateral system, but in that paper they put forward options for reconciling the proliferation of FTAs with genuine multilateral liberalization. The Wonnacotts propose that in the extension of NAFTA to a hemispheric FTA, a hybrid FTA (part FTA and part customs union) be established. Under the suggested arrangement, there would be a common external tariff for some products, along with customs union rules (required unanimity) for extending free trade relations with outside countries (also, obviously, no rules of origins for customs unions products). They would also eliminate rules of origin on all products where the FTA members have tariffs of less than 2 or 3 percent.

Regarding the future relations between the Western Hemisphere FTA and APEC—taking into account that some countries (the United States, Chile, Mexico) would be members of both organizations—rules would be established so that neither APEC nor the hemispheric FTA would be allowed to block the formation of the other. They would also allow any country in the Western Hemisphere FTA to join APEC if it so chose because they argue that this would not cause large-scale trade

144

diversion (while allowing APEC nations to join an expanded NAFTA would potentially cause such diversion).

Their main goal in this proposal, they state, is to mitigate the problems associated with hub-and-spoke systems and to remove the burdens imposed by rules of origin. These are worthy goals, but the resulting system—not to say the immense problems associated with timing and implementation—is a complicated patchwork of differing trade rules, rights, and obligations. To revert to the original example, imagine a bureaucrat or a corporate planning department trying to sort out the basic rules of commerce in the year 2005 for a system that consists of regional arrangements replete with customs union rules, individual FTA rules, overlapping bilateral agreements, and particular rules for nations belonging to both APEC and an expanded NAFTA. The Wonnacotts' effort is a commendable exercise, but the end result truly demonstrates the efficient practicality of returning to a single table of negotiations in Geneva.

Regional Trade Initiatives

At the end of 1995, the United States, in the words of *Wall Street Journal* reporter Bob Davis, found itself "up to its ears in free trade pacts." Without a great deal of thought about the implications—both economic and political—of its commitment, the Clinton administration has committed the United States to sweeping preferential trade arrangements with both East Asia and Latin America. In Latin America, the Miami Summit of the Americas pledged to complete negotiations for a hemispheric free trade arrangement by the year 2005; and in East Asia, the United States and the other APEC nations committed themselves to achieving free trade in the trans-Pacific region by the year 2010 for developed countries and 2020 for less developed countries within the region. This section will describe in more detail the sequence of events leading to these new regional trade commitments, and will describe the reaction of the EU to these regional initiatives. One point should be underscored, however: with the exception of the move toward European unity (which envisioned a full-scale political entity at the end of the road), these regional integration plans dwarf previous regional initiatives and present unprecedented challenges to the multilateral trading system.

The Move to Hemispheric Free Trade

The U.S.-Canada Free Trade Agreement in 1988 and the onset of the NAFTA negotiations in 1989 coincided with a resurgence of economic growth and renewed confidence in Central and South American countries. Simultaneously, this triggered a new wave of bilateral and subregional free trade negotiations, the most important being MERCOSUR, the revived Andean Pact, CACM (the Central American market), and CARICOM (the Caribbean nations' market), as well as a series of bilateral negotiations and signed agreements. These include alliances between Mexico and Chile, Mexico and CACM, Chile and Venezuela, Chile and Colombia, Venezuela and CACM, and CARICOM with Colombia and Venezuela.

In 1990, President George Bush put forward his Enterprise for the Americas program that envisioned a future hemispheric free trade agreement. President Clinton embraced the essential elements of the Bush proposal, and in December 1994, the United States hosted the Summit of the Americas conference, at which the leaders of thirty-four Latin American governments committed their countries to the goal of a free trade area for the hemisphere. The year 2005 was established as the deadline for completion of negotiations leading to a removal of tariffs and other barriers to trade. In a separate announcement at the summit, the United States, Canada, and Mexico invited Chile to enter into negotiations to join NAFTA (*International Trade Reporter* December 14 and 20, 1994).

Despite the high expectations that came out of the Miami summit, the events of 1995 raised substantial doubts and obstacles to moving rapidly toward hemispheric integration. First, within weeks of the Miami declaration, the collapse of the Mexican economy shook public opinion in the United States and dampened enthusiasm in Congress for additional trade liberalization—particularly among the incoming freshmen Republicans who were already skeptical of U.S. foreign political and economic ventures (see below for more details on the new politics of trade).

Second, in 1995 the Clinton administration and the new Republican majority in Congress were at loggerheads over renewal of the fast-track authority under which trade agreements are voted up or down within a certain time without amendment. Weakened by large-scale Democratic losses in the 1994 midterm elections and thrown back on its bedrock labor and environmental constituencies, the Clinton administration demanded the authority to negotiate new side environmental and labor agreements as a part of new fast-track authority. Republicans, as they had been before becoming a majority, were adamantly opposed to granting such authority. In addition, by the end of 1995, presidential politics became a factor, and Republicans were reluctant to allow the president to reap the potential benefit from a free trade agreement with Chile. Thus, a stalemate will continue at least until after the 1996 presidential election.

MERCOSUR. Meanwhile, events in Latin America had moved forward, independent of U.S. politics and trade policy. The most important new experiment in economic integration is the Southern Common Market (MERCOSUR), combining the economies of Brazil, Argentina, Uruguay, and Paraguay. Created in 1991, MERCOSUR, with a combined GDP of more than $700 million and a population of 200 million, represents more than 50 percent of the Latin American market. In 1994, global exports of the MERCOSUR countries totaled $63 billion and global imports almost $59 billion, of which around 30 percent were capital goods (Ahearn 1995b).

Clearly, both by size and by historic tradition, the nations of MERCOSUR (at least Brazil and Argentina) represent the most important actors in determining future South American political and economic policies. For the most part MERCOSUR is now a fully functioning free trade area—as of January 1, 1995, 85 percent of trade among the four nations became duty free, and a common external tariff (CET) was also established for about 85 percent of imports from outside countries. For both the zero tariff and the CET there were important sectoral exceptions, such as automobiles, computers, capital goods, textiles, and sugar. And together as a customs union group, the four nations of MERCOSUR are in the process of negotiating zero-tariff agreements with Bolivia, Peru, Ecuador, Colombia, and Venezuela. Chile became a member in 1996.

Further, as noted above, there are other important trade agreements proposed as well as completed among hemispheric countries, including those of Mexico with Costa Rica, Chile, and the Andean Pact nations; CARICOM with Venezuela and Colombia; and Chile with Canada. Then, in December 1995, the EU signed an agreement with fifteen Latin American foreign ministers to begin the process of negotiating eventual free trade agreements between the two groups of nations. It should be noted that the EU as a whole is a more important trading partner for Brazil and Argentina, the two largest South American economies, than is the United States (*International Trade Reporter* December 13, 1995).

Future Scenarios. The Miami summit agreed to an action plan to achieve the goal of free trade in the hemisphere, but it left open the negotiating framework for achieving this end. Two different approaches are currently on the table. Under one approach, the negotiating process would harmonize the disparate elements of existing bilateral and subregional trade agreements through a baseline set of negotiations that derive largely from the structure of NAFTA: in effect, existing subregional groups would be expected to adopt timetables for accepting NAFTA-equivalent obligations. This is the method favored by the United States.

Under an alternate scenario, favored strongly by Brazil but with support also from other South American countries, emphasis in the immediate future would be placed on deepening and expanding (non-NAFTA) subregional agreements such as MERCOSUR and the Andean Pact. Only later would direct negotiations regarding the more sweeping liberalization provisions of NAFTA be undertaken (Ahearn 1995b).

There are three factors behind the support for the second scenario. In the first place, Brazil retains a strong desire, through history and its economic significance in the region, to be a political and economic counterbalance to the United States. Brazil and other Latin American countries are also aware that they will be in a stronger negotiating position if they consolidate subregional alliances before facing the United States in future trade negotiations.

Second, and linked to the first factor, is that for both Brazil and Argentina the EU (and not the United States) is a more important trading partner. The United States is the destination for only 20 percent of Brazil's exports and 9 percent of Argentina's exports. Thus, both countries have reason to move MERCOSUR toward a special relationship with the EU—one that is not complicated or made more difficult by a hemispheric FTA.

Third, not only for Brazil but also for other Latin American nations, there are a number of "sensitive" sectors and issues where the preference is to stretch out change and liberalization. These include questions relating to intellectual property, government procurement, services, and harmonization of competition policy.

In keeping with the more general arguments advanced in this chapter, U.S. and ultimately world economic welfare are more likely to be advanced by the Brazilian-led second option. The somewhat slower pace of change will be counterbalanced by the potential for a more varied and flexible system of trade alliances—particularly if the EU follows through on its Latin American initiative—that will decrease the chance that entrenched regional trading blocs will become obstacles to further multilateral liberalization in coming years. In addition, MERCOSUR and the Andean Pact countries should strongly consider adopting the liberalization strategy that is emerging in APEC (see below): that is, moving forward on a WTO-compatible unconditional MFN basis as a safeguard against jeopardizing developing ties with the EU and East Asian nations such as Japan, Korea, and Taiwan, which have already demonstrated a keen interest in increased investment and trade with Latin America.

APEC and the Regional U.S. Focus

Though the idea of a Pacific economic cooperation group has been around since the 1960s, it was not until 1989 that an institutional focus was achieved with the creation of the Asia Pacific Economic Cooperation group, sparked by an initiative by then-Australian Prime Minister Bob Hawke.

At the first meeting in Canberra, the APEC trade ministers agreed to a set of principles to develop closer trade ties based on recognition of diversity within the region, on agreement by consensus, and on informal consultations rather than formal trade negotiations. As a corollary, it was agreed that the organization would not evolve into a trading bloc.

As noted above, it was the Clinton administration that moved to change the focus and goals of APEC from an informal consultative mechanism to a more formal organization promoting trade liberalization—and ultimately preferential trade arrangements—within the Pacific region. At the fifth annual meeting in November 1993, President Clinton called for a strengthening of the organization and the formation of a Committee on Trade and Investment that would "create a coherent APEC perspective and voice on global trade and investment issues and increase cooperation among members on key issues." The most concrete trade liberalization step taken at Seattle was the commitment to develop a voluntary, nonbinding investment code for the region.

In November 1994, in Bogor, Indonesia, the APEC nations, again after U.S. prodding but with crucial support from President Suharto of Indonesia, took a much larger step of agreeing to the goal of free trade and investment in the Asia Pacific region by the year 2020. The developed countries in APEC promised to attain the same goal by the year 2010. In addition, the Bogor Declaration committed the APEC nations to explore the creation of a voluntary dispute mediation service "to supplement the WTO dispute settlement mechanism, which should continue to be the primary channel for resolving disputes" (Bogor Declaration, 7).

The 2020 (2010) APEC free trade goal was only that: a goal. Though the APEC heads of state directed their ministers to "begin preparing detailed proposals for implementing [the] present decisions," no guidelines were established for such a blueprint. In reality, as events in 1995 demonstrated, any attempt to create such a road map would raise fundamental questions about the structure and purpose of APEC—questions that the leaders at Bogor left unanswered.

Run Up to Osaka. During 1995, as plans for the December APEC meeting in Osaka took shape it became increasingly clear that APEC faced crucial decisions regarding the implementation of its free trade goals—and that these decisions would irrevocably shape the nature of the organization and its relation to other nations in the multilateral trading system. The situation was remarkably similar to that faced by the United States and the nations of Latin America in implementing the free trade for the Americas goal; and once again an American vision for implementation was pitted against a competing local (Asian) vision of how to proceed.

The United States, supported largely by Australia and New Zealand (hence the term the "Anglo-Saxon vision"), pushed for clear rules and targets that would be binding in much the same manner as WTO rules are binding. The U.S. vision foresees detailed annual negotiations leading to fixed commitments covering all trade (and ultimately investment) sectors. Though never fully articulated, the creation of a binding dispute settlement system is a necessary adjunct to the U.S. plan. The underlying assumptions of the U.S. perspective were adopted and most cogently articulated by the Eminent Persons Group (EPG), led by U.S. economist Fred Bergsten. The EPG, particularly in its 1994 annual report, set forth the case for a rules-oriented, reciprocity-based framework for future APEC negotiations and decisions (APEC 1994). In an early version of the report the EPG also called for a detailed, quite legalistic dispute settlement system—this was diluted in the final version of the report.

As in Latin America, there is a competing scenario for the future of APEC, embodied in the so-called "Asian way." Led cautiously (so as not to anger the Americans) by Japan, the Asian members of APEC have successfully countered the U.S. vision and pressed the view of APEC as a "consensus building" organization that will allow each nation voluntarily to adopt separate paths to trade liberalization—"concerted unilateralism" is the term used to describe this negotiating system. "APEC is not based on contracts and treaties," stated a top Japanese trade official to the *Economist* magazine—or, as a *Washington Post* writer wrote, "No pushy lawyers, please. We're settling things the Asian way" (*Economist* 1995; *Washington Post* 1995).

At Osaka, clearly the "Asian way" carried the day—"Japan Conquers APEC," headlined the *Economist*. No timetables or deadlines were adopted, and each APEC nation was asked to provide its first "down payment" in trade liberalization at the next annual meeting in the Philippines in December 1996. "Consensus" and "flexibility" were the operative terms for future liberalization—though it should be noted that the United States successfully stopped a retrograde move to exempt certain sensitive sectors from the free trade commitment.

The crucial question of MFN—left unanswered even after Osaka—was, What is "open regionalism," and what is the policy behind the term, that APEC will ultimately adopt regarding the multilateral principle of most favored nation. To some, open regionalism means opening any APEC liberalization on an unconditional MFN basis to all other nations—representatives of Japan and Korea have voiced strongest support for this principle. To others, and certainly to the United States, open regionalism has a more limited application, in that APEC would be open to outside nations but only on the basis of reciprocity.

Statements of most Asian leaders show that they are proceeding on the assumption that their individual plans for liberalization will be taken unilaterally and will extend to all trading nations. The United States, while it has made no definitive announcement, is likely to demand strict reciprocity for any market-opening policies it puts in place. The EPG, in its 1994 report, made the case for reciprocity and argued that unilateral measures would have to be supplemented by detailed reciprocal negotiations beyond a certain point. For a recent view of the Osaka proceedings by an EPG leader, see Fred Bergsten (1996); for the counter view, which also documents the amount of unilateral liberalization already undertaken by East Asian economies, see the Saxonhouse chapter in this volume. U.S. Trade Representative Mickey Kantor insisted at Osaka that whatever the negotiations will produce in the future, there should be "no free riders" (Kantor 1995).

Finally, one political point should be added. The Clinton administration's commitment to institute free trade within APEC by the year 2010, while allowing China, with whom the United States now runs a $30 billion trade deficit, a free ride until the year 2020 is politically unsellable to the U.S. Congress—no matter which party is in control. Should APEC negotiations go forward, this portion of the Bogor Declaration will certainly have to be renegotiated.

Europe—A North Atlantic Free Trade Area?

For a number of reasons, outside observers have until recently assumed that Europe would not be interested in advancing trade liberalization through bilateral or regional trade agreements (with the exception of agreements in its backyard, Eastern Europe). First, in the early 1990s, even before the Uruguay Round was completed, a number of European countries were plagued with the lingering effects of a prolonged recession. In addition, EU member nations were preoccupied with implementing the far-reaching decisions at Maastricht and in planning for a major constitutional conference in 1996. Finally, what thinking there was about additional trade agreements was largely confined to dealing with issues related to the emergence of capitalist economies in Eastern Europe and the implications for EU trade and investment policy.

Over the past six to nine months, however, possibly spurred by the rapidly moving regional trade initiatives in Asia and Latin America, EU officials have reversed course and signaled an increasing interest in exploring additional bilateral and regional free trade agreements.

Calls for negotiating a North Atlantic free trade agreement first came from Canadian Prime Minister Chretien, but in the spring of 1995 EU Trade Minister Sir Leon Brittan, British Prime Minister John Major, German Foreign Minister Klaus Kinkel, and other high-ranking European officials have endorsed such a proposal. The U.S. response has varied from cautious to skeptical. In early June, Secretary of State Warren Christopher, in a Madrid address, espoused the idea of U.S.-EU negotiations on a variety of individual areas but stopped short of advocating a full-fledged free trade agreement. In earlier comments, Commerce Under Secretary Jeffrey Garten was more positive, endorsing the general idea of stronger North Atlantic ties, but Deputy U.S. Trade Representative Charlene Barshefsky stated on May 26 that while the United States was interested in exploring bilateral talks to remove barriers in specific sectors—telecommunications, investment, agriculture—these talks would "not necessarily" lead to a free trade area (*International Trade Reporter* April 23, May 3, and June 7, 1995).

During the fall of 1995, two events gave greater impetus to closer and more formal U.S.-EU trade and investment ties. In mid-November, under the auspices of the European Commission and the U.S. Department of Commerce, a summit of U.S. and EU business leaders met and adopted a number of initiatives and recommendations to their respective governments, including increased harmonization of technical and product standards, acceleration of tariff cuts agreed to in the Uruguay Round, and greater effort to solve the leftover Uruguay Round issues in telecommunications and financial services. Then, on December 2, political leaders of the United States and the EU formally agreed to the recommendations on technical and product standards, and to cutting tariffs on information technology immediately (*Financial Times* 1995a and b).

In addition to trade liberalization discussions with the United States, the EU is moving in other ways to signal its readiness to advance trade reform both bilaterally and multilaterally. In December

1995, the EU signed an accord with MERCOSUR that will lead to negotiations toward a free trade agreement in future years, and it has
adopted more formal trade negotiating ties with other nations of South
America, particularly Chile. In Asia, the EU held a formal trade and
investment summit with a group of East Asian nations in March 1996,
and in 1995 it agreed to formal annual meetings on economic issues
with Japan (*Korea Times* 1995).

Finally, of course, the EU is moving ahead with bilateral trade
agreements with nations in its own backyard of Eastern Europe. It
signed so-called Europe Association Agreements with Czechoslovakia,
Hungary, and Poland in 1992, and with Romania and Bulgaria in 1993.
The agreements assume "vaguely" (Winters 1994) that these nations
will eventually become full members of the EU, but in the interim the
agreements provide the means for lowering barriers between the individual countries and the EU. They have been a mixed blessing for the
East European nations, and they have caused some problem for outside nations such as the United States. Some commentators (Winters
1994), while acknowledging some advances toward liberalization, have
labeled the agreements a "missed opportunity," pointing to their defi-
ciencies in failing to lower barriers for key East European commodities
such as textiles, steel, and agricultural products, and for continuing to
subject these countries to the threat of antidumping actions in their
central export sectors. In addition, substantial trade diversion is likely
to result from the agreements, and it is this fact—even an increase of
tariff rates for some outsiders—that has propelled the United States
and other nations to protest some of the provisions of the Association
Agreements.

The reappearance of the EU as a major factor in bilateral and regional trade liberalization negotiations during 1995 is a factor of crucial
importance. With the EU signaling its willingness to take additional
steps—in Asia, North America, and South America—to liberalize trade
and investment, the case for avoiding a plethora of discriminatory preferential trading arrangements has become much stronger. Proponents
of U.S.-centered regional hub-and-spoke systems can no longer argue
that such moves are necessary because a multilateral negotiation is impossible in the near term.

The U.S. Political Climate against Further Liberalization

Before arguing the case for the multilateral alternative to a world of
overlapping and competing multilateral arrangements, we must assess
the current political realities relating to trade politics in the United
States. And in candor, it should be stated immediately that these reali-

153

ties will have a negative effect on any course suggested for further liberalization—whether on a bilateral, regional, or multilateral basis.

In assessing the political climate in the United States regarding further trade liberalization, one must first go back to the NAFTA debate, which opened deep divisions within the U.S. political community. These divisions have widened, even though NAFTA itself passed in the Congress by substantial margins.

Despite the NAFTA (and later GATT) victories, two forces opposed to trade liberalization remain formidable: Ross Perot and the labor-environment left wing of the Democratic Party. After the 1994 congressional elections, the labor-environmental wing of the Democratic congressional delegation, headed by Rep. Richard Gephardt (D-Mo.) was greatly strengthened; Democratic losses came largely from the suburbs and from the South, both traditionally more protrade. With the Clinton administration divided on new trade initiatives, this wing of the party is asserting itself independently—as evidenced by Rep. Gephardt's call for a U.S. Business Code of Conduct for international trade, including a commitment to stringent new labor and environmental rules. President Clinton has moved to accommodate his labor and environmental constituencies by demanding that all new trade agreements contain environmental and social charter provisions.

As for the Republicans, while the leadership of the party remains committed to free trade, there is a growing nationalist wing that views all U.S. international commitments with suspicion. Though the journalist and potential presidential candidate Patrick Buchanan represents only a small minority sentiment within the party, the Buchanan-Perot alliance against GATT forced congressional Republicans to agree to an independent commission that will review WTO dispute settlement decisions to determine whether they are in the U.S. national interest. Freshmen Republicans in the House will be a key barometer. Initial indications suggest that these Republicans are not anti–free trade but are highly nationalistic and susceptible to Perot-like demands that the United States no longer tolerate alleged free riding on trade rules by other nations.

In this situation, the timing of the Mexican peso crisis could not have been more unfortunate. Despite the overwhelming support for NAFTA from Republican economists and from all former Republican presidents, the first major international economic crisis faced by new Republicans in Congress has resulted in at least a $50 billion bailout, of which $20 billion must come from the U.S. Treasury—and the end may not be in sight. Whatever the final outcome on Mexico, presidents in the future, whether Republican or Democrat, will face a more skeptical, questioning Congress when they call for additional trade liberalization.

For the immediate future, given the split in the Democratic Party and the Clinton administration's demand that new trade negotiating authority contain provisions for labor and environmental agreements—a demand that is anathema to the Republicans—no major new trade initiatives seem possible until after the 1996 U.S. presidential elections.

What Is to Be Done?

Contrary to the general view of the trade policy community in Washington, this chapter argues that the pause in large-scale trade negotiations until 1997 may well have fortunate consequences. It will allow leaders both in the United States and among the nations of East Asia and Latin America to stand back and assess more realistically the potential negative consequences of a "spaghetti bowl" world of overlapping bilateral and regional trade agreements. In Latin America, the interests of the continent are best served by the Latin American nations' first getting on their feet and then negotiating from greater strength with the "colossus of the North." In Asia, the passage of time will allow Japan, if it can summon the will, to build a coalition in APEC against the creation of a reciprocity-based preferential trading agreement. Finally, assuming that EU leaders retain the political capacity to move forward with bilateral and regional trade initiatives, the resulting potential mixture of crosshatched trade arrangements—with a myriad of rules of origin and tariff rates—will make it ever easier to make the case for going back to a single negotiating table in Geneva.

Despite the political weakness of the Clinton administration on trade issues and the divisions within the free trade coalition in the United States, steps can and should be taken to prepare for future trade liberalization. At a minimum, the Clinton administration should signal to major U.S. trading partners that the time has come to begin planning for future multilateral negotiations, the timing of which will depend on political conditions in the United States and in the major trading nations around the world.

Quiet diplomacy is called for, particularly among the G-7 nations, the APEC leaders, and the largest economies in Latin America, such as Brazil, Argentina, and Mexico. Because the United States blundered at the 1994 G-7 meeting by springing a proposal for new multilateral negotiations without consultation, it must now proceed cautiously; but it might be possible to get an agreement this year for a G-7 study group to formulate a tentative agenda for a new round within the next few years. Once again, 1997 is a logical target for such a decision, for by that time the U.S. presidential election will be over, and the EU will have concluded its seminal 1996 constitutional conference and will have reached major decisions regarding the future of a federal state for Europe.

High on the agenda for new multilateral negotiations—along with competition policy, investment, the environment, and other issues—should be reform of the GATT Article XXIV rules regarding customs unions and FTAs. As noted earlier in this chapter, the trading world is experiencing a new wave of multilateral trade treaties, and by common consent the existing Article XXIV rules are inadequate to protect the multilateral system from discriminatory trade diversion.

This chapter is not the place to make a single recommendation regarding Article XXIV reform, but among the suggestions already put forward, the following are of particular note. First, nations entering into regional arrangements should be obligated to submit to full surveillance by the new WTO trade policy review mechanism. The WTO should have the authority to monitor and trace trade patterns by sector and industry both before and after a treaty is signed in order to assess trade diversion—and to issue rulings dictating changes in regional agreements or compensation for injured parties.

In addition, the WTO should consider prescribing that for new FTAs or customs unions, the member nations agree to adopt the lowest tariff or the most liberal trade or investment rule among their members as the baseline for the treaty (see Bhagwati 1994). Further, there should be some mechanism by which, after a certain period, the terms of the regional arrangement would be opened to all WTO members on an unconditional MFN basis. This suggestion represents a compromise between those who oppose additional FTAs and those who argue that because of the free-rider problem it will be impossible to get nations to agree to extend immediately to all nations their negotiated concessions.

Assuming that after several years there is no consensus for a new WTO trade round, rather than proceeding with overlapping FTAs around the world as the Clinton administration intends, the United States should revert to former U.S. Trade Representative William Brock's call for GATT-plus negotiations—a call to any nation in any region to join in a multilateral negotiation for further liberalization. A similar proposal has been advanced by Canadian Trade Minister Roy McLaren (1995).

This worst case scenario, however, may well be avoided. During the early months of 1996, a succession of voices, both in the United States and other countries, raised increased concerns about the drift to regional trading blocs and all that such a movement portended. In February 1996, Renato Ruggiero, the director general of the WTO, suggested that the members of the WTO consider establishing a deadline of 2010 for a global free trade pact. Several months later, Donald Johnston, the incoming secretary general of the OECD, strongly supported Ruggerio's recommendation for a deadline and timetable (*International Trade Reporter* March 20, 1996; *Financial Times* June 3, 1996).

Their statements were echoed by prominent academic trade policy analysts, such as Fred Bergsten of the United States, head of the Institute for International Economics and a leader in the movement over the past several years to give high priority to APEC; and Martin Wolf of Great Britain, associate editor of the *Financial Times* and a longstanding critic of regional trading arrangements (*Foreign Affairs* May/June 1996, 105–20; and *Financial Times* February 27, 1996).

In the end, much will depend on the trade policy of the winner of the 1996 U.S. presidential elections and on his ability to persuade the American electorate and a skeptical Congress that free trade on a global basis is in the interest of the United States. While other nations and the leaders of multilateral trade organizations can help to develop momentum for future multilateral trade and investment liberalization, only U.S. leadership can produce concrete results.

References

Ahearn, Raymond J. "Andean Pact—U.S. Trade Relations: Evolution and Prospects." *CRS Report to Congress*, Congressional Research Service, Library of Congress, 1995a.

———. "MERCOSUR-U.S. Trade Relations, Evolution and Prospects." *CRS Report to Congress*, Congressional Research Service, Library of Congress, 1995b.

Anderson, Kym, and Hope Norheim. "History, Geography, and REgional Economic Interpretation. In Anderson, Kym, and Richard Blackhurst, eds. *Regional Integration and the Global Trading System.* New York: St. Martin's Press, 1993.

APEC. *Achieving the APEC Vision: Free and Open Trade in the Asia Pacific.* Second Report of the Eminent Persons Group, August 1994.

Barber, Lionel. "U.S.-EU Accord Aims to Cement Transatlantic Ties." *Financial Times,* December 3, 1995.

Barfield, Claude. *The Ties That Bind: The United States and Europe.* Trans Atlantic Partnership, Washington, D.C., 1992.

———. "U.S.-China Trade and Investment in the 1990s." In James Lilley and Wendell Willkie, eds., *Beyond MFN: Trade with China and American Interests.* Washington, D.C.: AEI Press, 1994.

Bergsten, Fred. "The Case for APEC." *Economist*, January 6, 1996.

Bhagwati, Jagdish. "Regionalism and Multilateralism: An Overview." In J. de Melo and A. Panagarya, *New Dimensions in Regional Integration*. Cambridge: Cambridge University Press, 1994.

Bhagwati, Jagdish, and Anne Krueger. *The Dangerous Drift to Preferential Trade Agreements*. Washington, D.C.: AEI Press, 1995.

de Jonquieres, Guy, and Lionel Barber. "Business Meets to Revive U.S.-EU Ties." *Financial Times*, November 11, 1995.

Economist. "Japan Conquers APEC." November 11, 1995

Financial Times. November 15, 1995.

———. December 3, 1995.

———. February 27, 1996.

———. June 3, 1996.

Foreign Affairs. May–June 1996, pp. 105–20.

Government Printing Office. 1994 Economic Report of the President. Washington, D.C., 1994.

———. 1995 Economic Report of the President. Washington, D.C., 1995.

Jensen-Moran, Jeri. "Trade Battles as Investment Wars: The Coming Rules of Origin Debate." *The Washington Quarterly*, vol. 19, 1995, pp. 239–53.

Kantor, Mickey. *Financial Times*, December 1, 1995.

Khanna, Jane. "Asia-Pacific Economic Cooperation and Challenges for Political Leadership." Washington, D.C.: *Washington Quarterly*, vol. 19, 1995, pp. 257–75.

Korea Economic Institute of America. *AFTA after NAFTA*. Joint Korea-U.S. Academic Symposium, vol. 4, Washington, D.C., 1994.

———. *Economic Cooperation and Challenges in the Pacific*. Joint Korea-U.S. Academic Studies, vol. 5, Washington, D.C., 1995.

Korea Times, December 18, 1995.

McLaren, Roy. *Journal of Commerce*. March 7, 1995.

Noland, Marcus. "Implications of Asian Economic Growth." Institute for International Economics, Working Paper series, no. 94–5, Washington, D.C., 1995.

Panagariya, Arvind. "Should East Asia Go Regional?: No, No, and Maybe." World Bank, Policy Research Dept., WPS 1209, 1993.

———. "East Asia and the New Regionalism." *The World Economy*, vol. 17, 1994, pp. 817–39.

———. "The Free Trade Area of the Americas: Good for Latin America?" Forthcoming.

Preeg, Ernest H. *Trade Policy Ahead: Three Tracks and One Question*. Washington, D.C.: Center for Strategic and International Studies, 1995.

———. "Free Trade Across the Atlantic." *Journal of Commerce*, November 15, 1995.

U.S. Department of Commerce. "National Export Strategy." *Business America*, October 1994. *U.S. Government Printing Office, 1994.*

Washington Post. "APEC Pact Forged the Asian Way." November 18, 1995.

Winters, L. Alan. "Expanding LSC Membership and Association Accords: Recent Experience and Future Prospects." In Anderson and Blackhurst, *Regional Integration.*

Wolf, Martin. "Comments." In J. Schott, ed., *Free Trade Areas and U.S. Trade Policy.* Washington, D.C.: Institute for International Economics, 1989.

———. *Foreign Trade Highlights,* 1993.

Wonnacott, Paul, and Ron Wonnacott. "Liberalization in the Western Hemisphere: Challenges in the Design of a New Free Trade Agreement." Middleburg College, Working Paper no. 95-1, February 1995.

Yoshitomi, Masuru. "Developing a New International Division of Labor in East Asia and Building a New United States-Pacific Asia Relationship." Forthcoming.

Index

Ahearn, Raymond J., 147, 148
Andean Pact
    free trade negotiations under,
      146
    proposed common external tar-
      iff, 95
Anderson, Kim, 101n.19, 137, 141n1
APEC. *See* Asia-Pacific Economic Co-
    operation (APEC)
Argentina
    as member of MERCOSUR,
      147–48
    trade with EU, 148
Armington structure, 22
Asia-Pacific Economic Cooperation
    (APEC), 3
    Bogor meeting and Declaration,
      87, 101, 116–17, 149, 151
    Clinton proposals to change,
      149–51
    conditions in formation of, 108
    Eminent Persons Group, 112–13,
      121, 125, 129, 130n.21, 132, 140,
      150
    future relations with Western
      Hemisphere free trade agree-
      ment, 143–44
    as hub-and-spoke system, 87
    Nonbinding Investment Princi-
      ples, 117n.12
    open regionalism concept, 101–2
    Osaka meeting (1995), 55, 130–
      32, 150–51
    predicted outcome of free trade
      in, 87
    proposed free trade agreement,
      100–101, 112–13, 125
    resistance to Pacific preferential
      trading area, 121
    See also East Asian nations

Auto Pact (1965), U.S.-Canadian, 84,
    89

Bagwell, Kyle, 49n.57, 51
Baker, James, 111–12
Baldwin, Richard, 47, 49–50, 99
Barfield, Claude, 137
Barshefsky, Charlene, 152
Berglas, Eitan, 12n.12
Bergsten, C. Fred, 150, 151, 157
Bhagwati, Jagdish, 1, 2, 4, 5, 27n.29,
    30, 34, 35n.39, 38–39, 42n.47, 45–48,
    49n.56, 50, 51, 53nn.60, 61, 109nn.2,
    3, 141, 142, 156
Blackhurst, Richard, 141n.1
Bliss, Christopher, 46n.51
Bogor Declaration, 116–17, 131, 149,
    151
Brazil
    as member of MERCOSUR,
      147–48
    trade with EU, 148
Brecher, Richard, 2n.3
Brittan, Leon, 152
Brock, William, 156
Brown, Drusilla K., 115n.9
Buchanan, Patrick, 154
Bush administration
    concerns related to APEC,
      111–12
    Enterprise for the Americas, 79,
      109–10, 113, 146
    extension of NAFTA, 109
    trade policy shift, 45, 109–12

CACM (Central American Common
    Market), 146
Canada
    initiative in free-trade talks with
      U.S., 85, 152

161

participation in U.S.-Mexican free trade talks, 89
perceived disadvantage of customs union, 94
proposed bilateral preferential trade agreements, 108–9
trade agreements with United States, 81–86
U.S. proposed bilateral preferential trade, 108–9
Canada-U.S. Free Trade Agreement (CUFTA), 2
Caribbean Basin Initiative (CBI), 102
CARICOM (Caribbean Community), 146
Carr, Shirley, 85n.5
CES. See Constant elasticity of substitution (CES)
CET. See Common external tariff (CET)
Chile
EU trade negotiations with, 153
free trade with United States, 86
proposed inclusion in NAFTA, 89, 146
China, 151
Chrétien, Jacques, 152
Christopher, Warren, 102, 120, 152
Clinton, Bill
actions related to trade policy, 154
commitment to hemisphere-wide free-trade agreement, 79
trade facilitation agreement, 120
Clinton administration
APEC free trade policy, 151
commitments related to trade, 145
criticism of trade policy, 140–41
inclusions in proposed NAFTA extension, 142–43
multilateral free trade policy, 139–43, 155–56
open regionalism concept, 139, 150
policies related to APEC and NAFTA, 112–15
proposals to change APEC, 149–51
responsibilities related to trade, 155

trade policy, 130, 136, 139–43
trade policy toward China, 151
Colombo, John R., 83n.2
Common external tariff (CET)
across-the-board, 98–99
in customs unions, 93–96
implications for rules of accession, 98n.17
under MERCOSUR, 147
for nations in free-trade agreements, 93
in proposed Free Trade Association of the Americas, 79–80
in proposed hybrid free trade agreement, 143
Common markets
Caribbean Community (CARICOM), 146
MERCOSUR as, 146–47
as preferential trading areas, 4
See also European Union
Common-ocean arrangements, 42
Comparability, strict, 131
Constant elasticity of substitution (CES), 30–31
Continental trading arrangements, 42–43
Cooper, C. A., 2
Corden, W. Max, 86n.6
Cox, David, 84
Customs unions
characteristics of, 94
compared to free trade agreements, 92–99
hybrid system, 80
as preferential trading areas, 4
theory, 46–47
under WTO Article XXIV, 55

Davis, Bob, 145
Deardorff, Alan V., 47n.52, 115n.9
Dehejia, Vivek, 35n.39
De Melo, Jaime, 41n.45, 126, 128, 141n.1
Democratic Party, 154
Dhar, Sumana, 34n.36
Dornbusch, Rudiger, 86n.6
Drysdale, Peter, 101n.19

East Asian nations
APEC members' trade policies, 121–24

trade relations with EU, 118–19, 136–38, 153
trade relations with North America, 137–39
trade relations with United States, 137–38
Eastman, Harry C., 84
Eaton, Jonathan, 24n.24
Economic Cooperation among Developing Countries (ECDC), 4
Ellis, Howard S., 108
Eminent Persons Group. *See* Asia-Pacific Economic Cooperation (APEC)
Enders, Alice, 99
English, H. Edward, 84
Enterprise for the Americas proposal, 79, 109–10, 113, 146
European Community (EC), 1
  See also European Union (EU)
European Free Trade Association (EFTA), 2
European Union (EU)
  accord with MERCOSUR, 153
  interest in free-trade agreements, 152–53
  perception of APEC, 112–13
  regional trade initiatives, 118
  trade relations with Eastern Europe, 153
  trade relations with Japan and East Asian nations, 118–19, 153
  trade relations with South American countries, 153
  trade ties with United States, 152
  trade with Brazil and Argentina, 147–48
Europe Association Agreements, 153

Findlay, Ronald, 49n.57, 50, 96n.15
Frankel, Jeffrey, 34, 42, 96n.15, 118n.13
Free trade
  Clinton administration proposal for APEC, 151
  hub-and-spoke system with, 87
  scenarios for Western hemisphere, 147–48
  stumbling blocks and building blocks, 5

Free trade agreement, U.S.-Canadian
  as bilateral arrangement, 87–89
  changes related to NAFTA, 87–89
  negotiations, 85
Free trade agreements
  compared with customs unions, 92–99
  effect of rules of origin on small countries, 93
  negotiations for proposed, 141–42
  overlapping, 79, 87
  proposed hybrid, 79–80, 143–44
  rules of origin, 79–80, 91–93, 141–42
  U.S.-Chilean, 86
  U.S.-Israel, 102
  U.S.-Mexican negotiations, 85–86, 87–89
  when one economy dominates, 140–43
Free trade areas
  nontariff barriers, 98–99
  preferential trading areas as, 4
  under WTO Article XXIV, 55
  See also Customs unions
Free Trade Association of the Americas (FTAA), proposed
  with APEC free trade agreement, 101–2
  implications for Latin America, 86n.6
  institutional arrangements, 79–80
  with potential European free trade agreement, 101–3
FTAs. *See* Free trade agreements; Free trade areas
Funabashi, Yoichi, 112, 115n.10

Garnaut, Ross, 101n.19
Garten, Jeffrey, 152
General Agreement on Tariffs and Trade (GATT)
  Article XXIV: across-continent free trading areas, 43
  Article XXIV: preferential trading areas under, 1–2, 4, 43
  Article XXIV: proposed reform, 156

multilateral trade negotiations
under, 108–9
non-Article XXIV preferential
trading areas, 43
purview related to PTAs, CUs,
and Common Markets, 4
regional trading arrangements
under, 56–73
Uruguay Round, 143–44, 151
Generalized System of Preferences
(GSP)
preferences of MFN Article I, 55
regional preferences under, 35
Gephardt, Richard, 154
Gonzalez, Felipe, 120
Granatstein, J. L., 83n.2
Grossman, Gene, 20n.20, 49n.57,
129–30

Haberler, Gottfried, 42n.48
Harris, Richard G., 84
Hawke initiative, 109–12, 149
Hegemons
centering of preferential trading
areas, 4
preferential trading agreements
among, 54
sequential bargaining, 52
See also Nonhegemons
Helpman, Elhanan, 20n.20, 49n.57,
129–30
Herin, Jan, 91n.12
Hub-and-spoke system
effect of rules of origin on, 93
with potential North American-
Europe free trade, 87
predicted for Asia-Americas free
trade, 87
preventing development of,
100–101
problems of, 89–90
solution to rules of origin problem, 80, 93
Hufbauer, Gary, 96n.14

Information Technology Agreement
(ITA), proposed, 120n.16
Interdependence, 137
Investment
in East Asia (1985–1994), 115–18

foreign direct, 137
interdependence defined by, 137
Irwin, Douglas, 49n.56
Israel, 108–9

Japan
EU trade relations with, 153
investment in East Asia, 115–18
investment in Europe, 137
trade liberalization of, 130
Jensen-Moran, Jeri, 142
Johnson, Harry G., 2, 29, 36
Johnston, Donald, 157
Jonquieres, Guy de, 102

Kaifu-Delors-Lubbers Declaration
(1991), 119
Kantor, Mickey, 151
Katz, Jules, 96, 100
Kemp, Murray C., 2n.3, 46
Kinkel, Klaus, 3, 120, 152
Krishna, Pravin, 2n.3, 4n.4, 47, 49n.57,
50
Krueger, Anne O., 20n.19, 27n.29,
86n.6, 91n.12, 96n.15, 141
Krugman, Paul, 4, 7n.7, 16n.15, 34, 47
Kuroda, Makoto, 115n.11

Lawrence, Robert Z., 5
Levy, Philip, 47, 50
Lipsey, Richard, 2, 9, 24, 29, 30, 89n.9
Lloyd, Peter J., 12n.12
Ludema, Rodney, 51
Lutz, Mark, 7n.7, 28–29

McLaren, Roy, 156
Major, John, 152
Manning, Robert A., 114n.7
Massell, B. F., 2
Matching external tariff, 80, 96
Mayer, 50
Meade, James, 2, 22
MERCOSUR (Mercado Común del
Cono Sur)
accord with EU, 153
as free-trade area, 147
free trade negotiations under,
146
as nonhegemon centered prefer-
ential trading area, 4
success of, 2

tariffs, 95
trade policy, 54–55
Mexico
    initiative in free-trade talks with
        U.S., 86
    in negotiations leading to
        NAFTA, 88–89
    perceived disadvantage of cus-
        toms union, 94
    peso crisis, 146, 154
    trade effects of NAFTA, 31
Miami Summit, 145, 146, 147
Most favored nation (MFN)
    absence of across-the-board CET,
        98
    in Clinton trade policy, 139, 151
    tariffs under rules of origin, 92
MTNs. See Multilateral trade negotia-
    tions (MTNs)
Mulroney, Brian, 85
Multilateral trade negotiations
    (MTNs)
    in dynamic analysis of preferen-
        tial trade areas, 43–46
    sequential bargaining argument,
        52
    American use of, 45
Mundell, Robert, 27
Munro, G. R., 94n.13
Murayama, Warren H., 87

Natural trading partners
    defined, 3, 16
    hypothesis, 6–7, 28–29
    volume-of-trade and transport-
        cost, 29
New transatlantic marketplace
    (NTM), 120
Noland, Marcus, 137
Nonhegemons
    centering of preferential trading
        areas, 4
    liberalizing with hegemon, 3
    preferential trading agreements
        among, 54–55
    sequential bargaining with hege-
        mons, 52
Norheim, Hope, 137
North American Free Trade Agree-
    ment (NAFTA), 2
    accession clause, 99–100

changes in U.S.-Canadian agree-
    ment with, 87–89
Clinton proposal to extend,
    113–16
extension of, 109
as hegemon centered preferential
    trading area, 4
historical background, 81–86
hub-and-spoke issue related to,
    87–89
impact on East Asian trade,
    114n.8
matching external tariffs under,
    97
potential trade effects, 19, 31
proposed expansion to include
    Chile, 89, 146
rules of origin, 115

Osaka meeting. See Asia-Pacific Eco-
    nomic Cooperation (APEC)

Palmeter, N. David, 91n.11
Panagariya, Arvind, 4n.4, 12n.12,
    24n.24, 26, 28n.30, 30n.31, 34,
    41n.45, 49n.57, 96n.15, 101n.18, 126,
    128, 139, 141n.1
Park, Yung C., 89n.9
Pastor, Robert, 86
Pena, Felix, 87
Perot, Ross, 154
Petri, Peter, 101n.19, 112
Polak, Jacques J., 34n.37
Preferential trading areas
    accommodation in GATT Article
        XXIV, 1–2, 4, 43
    as alternative to multilateral
        trade talks, 2–3
    defined, 4
    dynamic time-path analysis,
        41–52
    hegemon and non-hegemon cen-
        tered, 4
    imperfect-substitutes model,
        22–27
    incentive structure alternatives,
        46–52
    Krugman theory, 46
    non-Article XXIV, 43
    politics and proliferation of,
        52–54

proposed Enterprise for the
Americas, 109–10
recommendations related to,
54–55
regional and nonregional, 4
revival of theory of, 2–3
"spaghetti bowl" phenomenon,
53
American use of, 45
Viner theory and model of, 2,
8–11
WTO categories, 1n.1
See also Asia-Pacific Economic
Cooperation (APEC); Euro-
pean Union (EU); MERCO-
SUR; North American Free
Trade Agreement (NAFTA)
Primo Braga, Carlos A., 114n.8
Process multilateralism, 44
Protection
effect in preferential trade agree-
ment, 7
related to rules of origin, 141–42
against trade diversion, 35–36
U.S. demands for, 18–19
PTAs. *See* Preferential trading areas;
Trade agreements

Reagan administration, 109
Regional integration (Viner model),
8–11
Regionalism
drift to regional trading blocs,
156–57
open, 101–2, 139, 150
period of first, 1–2
period of second, 2
of some preferential trading
areas, 4
in U.S. trade policy, 112–13, 120,
136, 139–42
Richardson, M., 19
Riezman, Raymond, 12n.12
Rodrik, Dani, 41n.45, 126, 128
Ruggerio, Renato, 157
Rules of accession, 99–100
Rules of origin
absence in certain circumstances,
92–93, 96–98
avoidance, 97–100
effect of, 20

function and effect in free trade
agreements, 90–92, 141–42
NAFTA, 115
in proposed hybrid free trade
agreement, 80, 143
specification of, 91

Safadi, Raed, 114n.8
Santer, Jacques, 120
Saxonhouse, Gary, 109n.1, 112,
118n.13, 130n.20
Schott, Jeffrey, 96n.14
Shearer, R.A., 94n.13
Sinclair, Peter, 96n.15
Soesastro, Hadi, 113, 117n.12, 123
"Spaghetti bowl" world of trade
agreements, 3, 53–54, 96, 143, 155
Spence, A. M., 84
Srinivasan, T. N., 2n.3, 27n.29, 42n.46,
46n.51, 47
Staiger, Robert, 49n.57, 51
Stein, E., 42n.48
Stern, Paula, 114n.7
Stern, Robert M., 47n.52, 115n.9
Stykolt, Stefan, 84
Summers, Lawrence, 4, 6, 14, 16, 34,
139

Tariff revenue
under natural trading partners
hypothesis, 31
redistribution, 7, 18–19
revenue-seeking activities, 27–28
in Viner model, 8–17
Tariffs
under customs union agreements, 94–97
East Asian economies, 121–24
endogenous, 38–41
MERCOSUR negotiations, 147
most-favored nations, 92, 98
for nations in free-trade agreements, 93–94
in proposed alternative free-
trade areas, 97–100
reduction under free trade agreement, 94–96
setting under free-trade agreement, 90–91
See also Common external tariff
(CET); Matching external tariff

Trade
  creation and diversion in natural
    trading partners analysis, 29
  creation and diversion (Viner),
    4–11
  EU, North American, and East
    Asian patterns, 137–39
  proposed trading systems,
    97–100
  U.S.-Canadian historical rela-
    tions, 81–86
  See also Free trade
Trade agreements
  Latin America and the Carib-
    bean, 146
  proposed in Western hemi-
    sphere, 147
  U.S. Canadian Auto Pact (1965),
    85
  U.S. negotiations for bilateral
    preferential, 108
  See also Free-trade agreements;
    Preferential trading areas
Trade liberalization
  under APEC Bogor Declaration,
    116–17
  critique of Eminent Persons
    Group, 129
  in major East Asian economies,
    122–30
  opposition in United States to,
    154
  unilateral, 124–29
  U.S. view of East Asian, 129–30
Trade negotiations
  EU ties with Chile, 153
  forerunners of NAFTA, 88–89
  for proposed free-trade agree-
    ments, 141–42
  Uruguay Round bilateral, 109
  See also Multilateral trade negoti-
    ations (MTNs)
Trade policy
  Clinton administration, 45, 120,
    130, 136, 139–43
  Clinton commitments to prefer-
    ential trade, 145
  EU East Asian, 118–19
  future U.S., 157
  recent U.S., 121
  regionalism in U.S., 137–43

U.S. policy related to China, 151
U.S. shift in, 45, 139–43
Transatlantic Business Dialogue
  (TABD), 120
Transatlantic Free Trade Area
  (TAFTA), proposed, 3, 120
  See also New transatlantic mar-
    ketplace (NTM)
Transport-cost criterion, 29, 36–38
Tyson, Laura, 139

United States
  Caribbean Basin Initiative, 102
  degree of dependence on trade,
    136–37
  investment in Europe, 137
  as major players in trading re-
    gions, 136
  proposal for preferential trade
    with, 108–9
  role in APEC Eminent Persons
    Group, 149
  shift to preferential trading area
    policy, 2–3
  trade agreements with Canada,
    81–86
  trade policy (mid-1980s-1990s),
    121
  trade ties with EU, 152

Viner, Jacob, 2, 4–5, 7–8, 29
Vines, David, 96n.15
Volume-of-trade criterion, 29–36

Waite, Peter, 83
Wan, Henry, 2n.3, 46
Wei Sheng-Jin, 34, 42, 118n.13
Wellisz, Stanislaw, 50
White, David, 102
Winters, L. Alan, 42n.6, 153
Wolf, Martin, 48, 140–41, 157
Wonnacott, Paul, 7n.7, 28–29, 80n.1,
  84–85, 101n.19, 125, 144
Wonnacott, Ronald J., 80n.1, 84, 89n.9,
  99, 125, 144
World Trade Organization (WTO)
  Article XXIV, 55
  idea for multilateral system
    based on, 132'
  initial actions, 3
  PTA categories under, 55

suggestions for, 156–57
U.S. trade and investment policy
  under, 136
See also General Agreement on
  Tariffs and Trade (GATT)

Yeats, Alexander, 114n.8
Yeutter, Clayton, 87
Yoo, Jung Ho, 89n.9
Young, J. H., 94n.13

A Note on the Book

This book was edited by
Cheryl Weissman of the publications staff
of the American Enterprise Institute.
The figures were drawn by Hordur Karlsson.
The index was prepared by Shirley Kessel.
The text was set in Palatino, a typeface
designed by the twentieth-century Swiss designer
Hermann Zapf. Coghill Composition Company of
Richmond, Virginia, set the type,
and Edwards Brothers, Incorporated,
of Lillington, North Carolina,
printed and bound the book,
using permanent acid-free paper.

The AEI Press is the publisher for the American Enterprise Institute for Public Policy Research, 1150 Seventeenth Street, N.W., Washington, D.C. 20036; *Christopher DeMuth*, publisher; *Dana Lane*, director; *Ann Petty*, editor; *Leigh Tripoli*, editor; *Cheryl Weissman*, editor; *Jennifer Lesiak*, editorial assistant (rights and permissions).

www.ingramcontent.com/pod-product-compliance
Lightning Source LLC
Jackson TN
JSHW011936131224
75386JS00041B/1419